SEEKING *Faith*

SEEKING Faith

IS RELIGION REALLY WHAT YOU THINK IT IS?

by
Nathan Rutstein

Bahá'í
PUBLISHING
Wilmette, Illinois

Bahá'í Publishing
415 Linden Avenue
Wilmette, IL 60091-2886

Printed in the United States of America
on acid-free paper ∞

06 05 04 03 02 5 4 3 2 1

Library of Congress Cataloging-in-Publication Data

Rutstein, Nathan.
Seeking faith : is religion really what you think it is? / by
Nathan Rutstein.
p. cm.
Includes bibliographical references and index.
ISBN 1-931847-01-0 (alk. paper)
1. Bahai Faith. I. Title.
BP365 .R87 2002
297.9'3—dc21
2001035642

Cover and book design by Suni D. Hannan

CONTENTS

1. – Seeking Faith . . . 3
2. – The Search . . . 17
3. – The Need for a Spiritual Guide . . . 31
4. –What Is Religion Anyway? . . . 47
5. – The Gate . . . 61
6. – The Glory of God . . . 79
7. – The Promised Day . . . 99
8. – Our Spiritual Reality . . . 121
9. – The Purpose of Life . . . 143
10. – The Soul's Journey . . . 159
11. – The Oneness of Humanity . . . 171
12. – Embracing Oneness . . . 183
13. – Times of Change . . . 193
14. – A Unified World . . . 201
Notes . . . 215
Bibliography . . . 221
Index . . . 225

1
SEEKING FAITH

As a little boy I had many important questions that I held to myself because no one, including my parents, ever discussed such matters. I was afraid they would think I was strange for seeking answers from them, for all that seemed to matter in our household was making a decent living, having enough food stored away in case my father lost his job, and having a warm place to live. My parents felt fortunate to be living in the United States, having escaped unharmed from the czar's anti-Jewish pogroms in Russia and from the ravages of the Bolshevik revolution. Their primary concern was survival. At family get-togethers a favorite topic of conversation was how they had made their way to freedom with very little money. These were stories that had to do with the ways they had outfoxed the authorities in the different countries they traveled through en route to America. The stories always set off laughter, though there seemed to be an underlying current of hysteria; it was if they were saying, "Boy, am I lucky I made it out in one piece!"

There were only two books in our four-room apartment in the South Bronx. One had been won by my mother in a weekly lottery held by the local movie house. It was the letter *G* volume of an encyclopedia set. The other book had been purchased by my father, who never actually read it. I remember very clearly when he bought it. I was around nine at the time.

As a matter of fact, I recall being surprised at my father for buying the book, because he made a rule of never buying anything from door-to-door salesmen. This occasion was an exception because the salesman who sold the book to my father looked nothing like the peddlers he was accustomed to seeing—disheveled looking men, usually immigrants, pushing pants, lingerie, socks, and men's underwear. The book salesman was tall, blond, and blue-eyed and wore a finely pressed light blue suit with a perfectly ironed shirt and a golden tie. He was also polite, and when he spoke, I had the impression that he sounded like someone whose ancestors came over on the Mayflower. In retrospect, I think that when my father handed the man the money, he wasn't buying a book so much as he was trying to buy acceptance into what he felt was "real America."

Though I never read the book, I remember its title: *Watchtower*. I also remember some of the pictures inside, which showed smiling men and women who looked very much like the salesman, only they had wings instead of arms. About a year later I learned that the proper term for those figures was angels.

My friends and I were not interested in reading. None of us knew where the local library was. But we knew where the five-and-ten cent store was. It was a place where we sharpened our shoplifting skills. The first time I held a Bible (the Old Testament) was when everyone in our gang of eleven year olds placed his right hand on the holy book pledging never to squeal on the others if he were caught stealing. Though the ritual lasted about six months, I never actually opened the Bible.

You would think that school would have been the place where I would find the answers to my questions—at least some of them. But the classroom situation was too intimidating. Instead of gaining answers, I found myself coming up with more questions. This wasn't because I was being challenged intellectually at Public School Number 77.

I wasn't interested in memorizing multiplication tables or learning the difference between adjectives and adverbs. I was a dreamer. While the teachers addressed our class, I dreamed of searching for treasure in faraway places, hitting home runs like Joe DiMaggio or Hank Greenberg, or fighting injustice like the Green Hornet, the leading character of a popular radio program in the late 1930s. I dreamed of being like the boxer Joe Louis so I could stop people from calling me "Christ killer."

My daydreaming wasn't merely an exercise in wonderment: I really wanted to know what caused the rain and snow; I wanted to know what made the sun shine; I wanted to know what made the birds fly and the fish swim; I wanted to find a way to reach the moon. I wanted to know if there really was a God. Was there life after death? And why were there so many wars—so much killing and hating? Would it ever stop? The question that puzzled me most was: Why am I in this world? My curiosity couldn't be satisfied in the classroom because the things I wondered about were never mentioned by my teachers, and I was too scared to approach them anyway.

Maybe I wasn't searching hard enough, but I couldn't find the answers within the religion in which I was being brought up. My parents were less-than-devout followers of Judaism. On high holy days we would all dress up to attend services at the temple, but we would spend most of the time outside, showing off our new clothes and gossiping. It puzzled me to see that one of my uncles, who actually admitted that he didn't believe in God, would not miss a minute of the services. He would don the prayer shawl and read aloud from his prayer book, trembling as if he were the most pious rabbi facing the Western Wall in Jerusalem. When I asked my uncle why he did that, he said, "Because my father and his father did that. It is upholding family tradition, Stupid!"

The family member who had the most positive religious impact on me while I was growing up was my mother's mother. "She is a real Jew," my mother would always say. Looking back, I can understand why my mother would say that. I never heard Grandma Fanny say an unkind word about anyone. I never heard her complain about her health, even though she was not well during the last five years of her life. Bone cancer can be awfully painful. Compassion should have been my grandmother's name. When she heard that an Italian family living on her block didn't have enough food, she would leave a bundle of groceries once a week at the entrance to their apartment. This went on until the husband found a job. Grandma Fanny was one of the kindest persons I've ever known. Whenever she would visit us, she would always come bearing a shopping bag stuffed with gifts. Every one of Grandma Fanny's presents gave me immense pleasure. She seemed to know what would bring me joy. Yet despite her generosity, selflessness, thoughtfulness, and kindness, she, too, was unable to answer the questions that seemed to haunt me. All she would say was, "My child, you need to believe." Because of her loving spirit, I didn't dare engage in debate.

There was a period in the early stages of my life, especially during my teenage years, when I began to believe that I would never find the answers I sought. For a while my personal search was derailed by my passion for sports. My goal was to become a professional baseball player, and I was on a course that was leading me toward achieving it. At a special tryout sponsored by the Brooklyn Dodgers, I was selected to be part of their metropolitan all-star youth team. All who were chosen were considered top prospects, and it was a great honor to be among them. But when I was offered an opportunity to go to college on the Charles Mott scholarship (and not because I was an academic whiz), I took it. Sadly, it wasn't something my father thought I should pursue. He felt strongly that I should follow the suggestion of my school guidance counselor, who suggested that I seek a trade. I'll never forget her assessment of me: "Nathan, you are not college material."

She was wrong. Although it was true that I was being admitted to college because I could hit a baseball often and far, I took advantage of the opportunity and made good. In the last semester of my sophomore year I had an awakening. I discovered I had a passion for knowledge and found myself feeling confident that I could attain it. The door to all of the questions that I had closeted was open again. There was a huge university library at my disposal, and there were professors who were willing to listen to me. I found my courses in history, sociology, geography, biology, anthropology, and political science fascinating. I also discovered other students who were on a similar quest.

After many late-night discussions, I found myself forming a philosophy. I was leaning toward atheism and gravitating toward Marxism. I had become convinced that it was a waste of time trying to deal with abstract concepts such as God, the possibility of life after death, and creation. I had made up my mind to inquire about only those matters that could be investigated empirically. Contemplating abstract concepts was like trying to count the number of angels dancing on the head of a pin and was, I felt, a worthless exercise.

I became involved in politics at DePauw University. Adlai Stevenson was running against General Dwight Eisenhower in the 1952 presidential election, and I was an enthusiastic Stevenson supporter. I soon discovered that trying to drum up support for him at DePauw was like trying to break down a brick wall with a screwdriver. Most of the students there came from wealthy or upper-middle class suburban families who traditionally voted Republican. They found Stevenson's Democratic one-world views traitorous, while I found them refreshing. The internationalization of our planet, I believed, was the next logical step in the social evolution of humanity.

Evidently the great majority of voters didn't agree with me, because Eisenhower clobbered my hero. I was terribly troubled. I felt that, because Stevenson had failed in his presidential bid, America and the rest of the world were doomed. I believed that having a warrior at the helm of our nation during the Cold War was a prescription for global disaster. However, while I was listening to the election returns at the student center and feeling so discouraged, the source for many of the answers to the questions that I had given up on years before was presented to me. Two students were drawn to me, for they sensed my despair. They could see that something was troubling me deeply.

I responded to them favorably because they displayed a sensitivity that nobody else had ever shown toward me. Also, the fact that one was black and the other was white impressed me. On our campus there were no real interracial friendships. At that time the university had a policy of admitting only three or four black men each year. And none were eligible to be rushed by the fraternities that housed most of the male students. Furthermore, no black women were admitted.

As I looked at these two close friends, I wondered what allowed them to buck a deep-rooted social norm such as racial prejudice. I was also impressed with the fact that they didn't try to give me advice and didn't try to assure me that everything was all right. All they wanted to know was what was wrong. And when I told them, they listened intently, allowing me to vent my concerns and frustrations. As long as I had lived no one—not even my grandmother—had ever listened to me with such genuine interest.

Though my candidate had lost the election, I felt as if I had found a source of hope. Not wanting to lose that feeling, I sought out the two friendly young men. We became a threesome, even though some of my fellow athletes thought I was crazy for hanging out with a couple of geeks. What they didn't know was that my new friends had access to a treasure chest of knowledge that I couldn't find anywhere else on campus—a treasure chest that would open the way for me to find answers to the questions that had haunted me for so long.

As a result, today I know that there is a loving and caring God, and I have a very strong sense of purpose in life. I look forward to each new day because I'm optimistic about the future. Furthermore, I'm aware of what I have to do to help make sure that humanity reaches the promised day.

I now know why I, a young Jewish lad from New York City, ended up attending a Methodist university in rural Indiana. I needed to learn about an aspect of reality that was not taught by any of my professors, nor by any other professors on campus. These two students—one from Chicago, the other from Atlanta—drew me, through their kindness, into a world of understanding that I never knew existed. They did this by simply sharing their beliefs and their faith in the earnest hope of healing a broken heart without ever mentioning the subject of religion. It was only after I inquired why they were able—with such profundity, clarity, and humility—to answer questions that no one else was able to answer that they mentioned their membership in the Bahá'í Faith.

I was startled by my positive reaction to their ideas and beliefs. Although I had earlier embraced Marx's idea that "religion is . . . the opium of the people," I found myself reacting to my new friends with sincere interest. In fact, I began to ask more questions—not cynical questions, but honest, sincere questions—because my friends were open-minded and pure-hearted men. The things I heard launched me into genuinely exploring a world of which I had never before been aware. I began reading from the sacred writings of the Bahá'í Faith so I could understand the Bahá'í Faith for myself.

The things I read were magical. The effect that those divine words had on me and on others I met convinced me that personal transformation was indeed possible. I attended gatherings that I thought at first couldn't be real because they seemed too good to be true. I had never experienced such a variety of human diversity in one room. Not only were there men and women of different skin color, but there were also old and young, as well as people of different nationalities and religious backgrounds. I noticed an absence of pretense, of boasting, of backbiting, and this was refreshing. It wasn't as if these people didn't have problems; they did. But they talked about them with confidence that they would eventually solve them. I was even more impressed to see that they didn't feel sorry for themselves. On the contrary, they turned what outwardly seemed negative into something positive. Whenever they would reveal a personal problem, it would be expressed with a sense of curiosity about what they might learn from the situation. Facing one's problems was seen as an opportunity for spiritual growth.

I was so taken by the spirit at the Bahá'í gatherings that for a while I was attending meetings almost every night of the week. While the contrast between what I experienced in and out of the Bahá'í gatherings was great, it suddenly dawned on me that what I was experiencing among the Bahá'ís was the way humans were meant to live their lives.

As the Korean War was winding down, I was drafted into the U.S. Army and shipped to Okinawa. It was during war maneuvers, sitting in a foxhole and reflecting on the Bahá'í teachings on peace, that I decided to become a Bahá'í.

In the sacred writings of the Bahá'í Faith I discovered a treasure chest of wisdom and knowledge that helped me find answers to many of the questions that had haunted me as a child and as a young man, and more—especially questions such as What is a human being? How do I discover my true self? What is the purpose of life? And what is the meaning of the term "children of God"? In the following pages you, the reader, will find answers to those fundamental questions that could change your life as they did mine.

2
THE SEARCH

Most of us are searching for something important, something that will improve the quality of our lives. On a conscious level we may not know exactly what that something is, but we know deep down that there has to be an improvement.

Perhaps our uncertainty of what we need stems from a fear of thinking too deeply about the world's terrible condition. After all, sadness hurts, and no one relishes pain.

Sometimes, however, with the help of a close friend, we may uncover some of those buried desires which, if fulfilled, could make our lives more meaningful. What we usually find is the need to be happy and to live in comfort, in security, and in harmony with the world around us. We all want this. For many of us, this kind of happiness seems beyond our reach. But it can be attained, even during the difficult times in which we live.

Some people have found a way to fulfill this deep and insistent yearning. For them, the inevitable pain of living, the stresses and strains of daily life, become more bearable because they have a sense of where they are headed in life—a sense of purpose and direction that helps them maintain their equilibrium.

Often it is the lack of direction in our lives that troubles us the most. But when we gain a realistic understanding of who we really are as human beings and of our purpose in life, we can begin to find the way to our goal.

As animals, human beings are not very impressive. Many creatures on our planet are bigger, stronger, and faster, and some have greater stamina and live longer than we do. Yet they are total captives of nature, lacking in imagination and scope of vision. A monkey in India, for example, is incapable of knowing that there are monkeys in Africa. Unlike other creatures, we humans are aware of other members of our species who are living on other continents, and we are able to communicate with them in seconds.

Though an eagle can fly and we cannot, we are able to build airplanes, space shuttles, and rockets that race past the fastest bird. Though a fish can swim underwater unaided and we cannot, we can devise underwater craft that allow us to live in and explore the oceans, exploiting them for our benefit. An elephant can trample a hut, but with man-made explosives we can demolish a skyscraper or carve out the side of a mountain.

Our uniqueness in creation is manifested in other ways—ways that other creatures cannot even begin to appreciate. We can discover invisible elements and substances and harness energy from them. We can build bridges and tunnels to traverse formidable natural barriers. We can travel to the moon or into outer space. We can remove a cataract from an eye with a laser beam. We can compose a symphony.

We would do none of these things were it not for certain inherent yearnings within us. One is to know; another is to love and to be loved. These yearnings are evident even in infancy. The mother's embrace of her baby is an exchange that fulfills each one's need for love. When the infant discovers her mother's breast and nurses, she is not only fulfilling her need to be physically nourished, she is also fulfilling the need to know as well as the need to love and be loved. But these needs do not stop at the mother's breast. As the child matures, her need to know must be satisfied time after time. So must her need for love. If these needs are not met, she becomes frustrated, angry, perhaps even hostile. Although she may try to hide these emotions, they will probably surface from time to time, especially when she is under stress.

Even beyond our needs to know and to love, something else sets us apart from all other forms of life: our spiritual nature. While some people reject this aspect of human nature as pure fantasy, we all experience its effects from time to time. The joy we feel as a result of helping someone is evidence of our spiritual nature. Even the cynic will agree that this feeling is not the result of physical stimulation. In reality, the joy comes from expressing the divine attributes of selflessness and kindness that are inherent in each of us. Every time we express love, compassion, honesty, or kindness, we are expressing some aspect of our spiritual nature, which is comprised of all of the divine virtues within us. None of us, no matter how "evil" we may seem, is entirely devoid of these virtues.

We are born with both a physical nature and a spiritual nature. Development of both is necessary if we are to attain our full potential as human beings.

Our physical nature is the source of those instincts that we possess in common with other creatures of the animal kingdom—the drive for survival, the need for nourishment and sleep, the impulse to reproduce, and the desire to flee or to fight when endangered. As human beings, we have free will and are faced with choices. Without wisdom we make wrong choices. If not properly cared for, our bodies will perish sooner than they would if they were appropriately fed, exercised, clothed, and housed. And unlike animals, we do not know instinctively what is best to eat, how much we should sleep, or what kind of exercise is best for us. Fortunately, through the ages, wise individuals have learned a great deal and have provided the human family with a large body of knowledge about how to care properly for their physical selves. With the passage of time, more and more information about health is becoming available, and people today are living longer than their ancestors did.

For many of us, discovering and developing our spiritual self is more difficult than taking care of our physical self. This is probably because the spiritual nature is invisible and intangible, and we generally don't give much credence to things that cannot be described or experienced in a concrete way. In the past, even some of the most celebrated philosophers considered that which was immeasurable or unidentifiable as unworthy of serious thought. One problem with this kind of thinking is that previously invisible and unsuspected things are constantly being discovered. Atoms have always been composed of various subatomic particles, but scientists did not discover this fact until relatively recently. Clearly, the fact that something cannot be seen is no guarantee that it does not exist. But because of this tradition of denying our spiritual reality, it is not surprising that some of us find it difficult to accept its existence.

Despite whatever doubts we may have about the "realness" of our spiritual nature, it is indeed real, and its development follows a process that is similar in many respects to the development of our physical nature. The growth and development of both natures is dependent on guidance from wise teachers and healers. The chances of our discovering and developing our spiritual nature all by ourselves are slim, especially if we live in a materialistically oriented society that bombards us daily with television, radio, magazines, and street corner gossip. If we internalize the values of such a society, we can become spiritually disoriented and anxiety-ridden, and, tragically, our spiritual nature, which can liberate us from the snares of materialism and selfishness, can remain dormant within us.

From time to time an extraordinary spiritual teacher such as Moses or Jesus reminds us of our spiritual nature, explaining what it is, why it is important to us, and how to develop it. When we fail to heed his directions we allow our physical nature to dominate our spiritual nature, and we operate on a level that is beneath our capacity and our station as human beings. In some respects, when we operate in this way, we sink to a level that is lower than that of an animal, because when our spiritual nature is dominated by our physical nature, we fall prey to our own appetites and passions and lose touch with the very part of us that brings the greatest joy.

Without the tempering influence of a growing spiritual awareness, our human intelligence can be very dangerous. We become capable of devising and using systems and machines to carry out genocidal schemes, and we engineer crafty means of cheating and swindling our fellow human beings. We create powerful weapons that could destroy the world and engage in practices that harm or poison our environment. But spiritual growth shifts our focus in life, making us more caring and giving, leading us to use our intelligence to help others and improve our community's quality of life.

But how is this spiritual growth attained? It is easy to see that religious involvement has never been any guarantee of spiritual development, not even for members of the clergy. The pages of history are filled with crimes committed in the name of God, and this is a continuing reality. But this does not mean that religion itself is useless. This is an important distinction. Just as we would not stop using airplanes merely because some are used to drop bombs, we ought not to abandon religion merely because some adherents have strayed from its true purpose.

Religion is supposed to be a clear conduit conveying God's guidance to humanity. But when the conduit becomes clogged with dogma and ritual and polluted with the lust for power, it degrades into a man-made organization and loses its divine inspiration. When this happens, fear and fanaticism are often used to preserve the "rightful" image of the religion's leaders.

No wonder so many of us have become confused about the value of religion. Perhaps we have rejected it outright, or perhaps we are struggling to cling to it. We are assailed by doubts and do not know where to turn for answers to very private and crucial questions—questions we are afraid to ask even those we trust for fear of being ridiculed and ostracized by people we love. Some of us have directed our spiritual energies elsewhere, maintaining our membership in some religion in name only and rarely participating in the religious community to avoid feeling hypocritical.

Those of us who have been so soured by our religious experiences that we have become agnostics or atheists still have the need to believe in something. Our faith impulse has simply been rerouted, often into political and social causes that seem to show the way to better the lot of humanity. We join with enthusiasm and hope.

In time, however, the enthusiasm wanes and the future seems as bleak as it did before we joined the movement. Internal bickering, political maneuvering, backbiting, and lack of direction and vision discourage us; we may become cynical and drop out of the movement.

But we all need to believe in something, even those of us who are disillusioned. We continue to search, differently, perhaps, than before—more tentatively, more cautiously and subconsciously. But still we search.

Belief is not blind faith. It is a process involving knowledge, understanding, and love. The more knowledge we acquire about a given subject, the better we can understand it. The better we understand the subject, the easier it is for us to love it. As our love becomes more firmly established, we grow secure about the object of our love. Belief begins and deepens as we acquire more and more knowledge and understanding. When we stop learning, however, belief degenerates into superstition, and fear replaces love.

For many of us, belief needs to be directed at someone, usually some hero or heroine. We have lost faith in the heroes of the past, even in our spiritual leaders and prophets. We find the followers of the different faiths unable to act according to their prophets' teachings. Nothing seems to work right anymore. The world around us seems to be collapsing, and there is no one to save us. Some of us have simply given up, but many of us who have not are seeking a savior. Holy scriptures are studied for signs, sayings of ancient seers or modern philosophers are examined for clues. We vote or work for some new charismatic politician, hoping that this one will be the longed-for savior, the one who will make life better. But deep down we know that something is missing.

Opportunists take advantage of the times and proclaim themselves prophets. Instant heroes are born, and some sincere but naïve seekers may be seduced. Massive amounts of money and energy are expended by established faith communities to revive our waning interest. The glitter, the pageantry, the persuasive interpretation of scripture, the healing exhibitions and television and radio blitzes attract some. In the meantime, the world around them grows increasingly desperate and spiritually bankrupt.

Though the picture seems grim, we continue to search. It is as though our soul, that essential and spiritual part of us, compels us to keep searching for something to believe in despite the growing signs of moral decay and hopelessness around us. We know instinctively that our uniqueness in this world invests us with a station that we can neither fully understand nor fully ignore. We also know, either consciously or subconsciously, that there is some greater purpose to our existence, some greater meaning to our lives. We just have to find it.

3
THE NEED FOR A SPIRITUAL GUIDE

It can be difficult to be optimistic these days. Wherever we look, we can see signs of the moral decay of society. Institutions we were taught to trust—the foundations of our moral and social order—not only seem unable to curb the decay but also seem to be enveloped in it themselves.

The dangers that this moral decay represents to us and to people we care about are unprecedented. Never before has the world been in such a state of trouble and danger. Previously unimaginable acts of terror on September 11, 2001, proved a rude wake-up call to a part of the world that had felt immune to such danger. Though the Cold War is over and the threat of global nuclear disaster has lessened, a stockpile of nuclear weapons remains, and there is the threat of such weapons' falling into the hands of other governments, terrorist groups, or militias. Coupled with that threat is the newly alarming specter of germ or chemical warfare.

Many other problems have now come to the fore as well. There is the incalculable threat posed by unchecked pollution of the earth's environment and careless exploitation of its natural resources. There are the ill effects of chronic political instability, economic instability, longstanding intractable disputes over control of certain pieces of land, famine, illiteracy, the pandemic of AIDS, the spread of other new and terrifying diseases we do not know how to treat, rising crime rates, soaring divorce rates, the sexual exploitation of women and children—these are only a few of the widespread problems that are plaguing human society.

Clearly, humanity needs to find a way to begin to address the root causes of these and other problems. We need a way to purge hearts of hatred, a way to overcome prejudice. We need a system that will consistently dispense true justice, a way to unite the peoples of the world and responsibly use the earth's resources for the good of all. Treating each problem in isolation from all of the other problems may solve that problem, but only temporarily, if at all. It is not enough. We need a solution that will encompass all of the problems—something that will ensure the happiness and well-being of all humankind. In short, we are talking about the salvation and preservation of the entire human race.

This sounds like a lofty, idealistic, impossible goal. Thinking about it can be discouraging as long as we keep turning to existing institutions, systems, and approaches for solutions.

If we are looking to politics for solutions, we are going to be disappointed. More efficient bureaucracies and more productive economies are not going to be enough. There are so many crises for our political leaders to respond to that no time remains for them to devise balanced long-term goals or plans for the future. Also, existing political structures and processes seem ungainly and inefficient and force our leaders to continue thinking in ways that are unsuited to solving contemporary problems. We seem to be locked into courses of action and patterns of behavior that keep us from really dealing with our problems. Our political systems, if we think about them objectively, seem inherently corrupt and divisive because they rely on practices such as patronage, lobbying, and campaigning—all of which are ways of attempting to gain advantage for one individual or group at the expense of others. Such practices make it all but impossible for the political process to produce substantial changes that are truly for the good of all. Politics is incapable of ensuring the salvation and preservation of the human race because it does not address the root cause of all of the problems: the steadily decaying spiritual health of human society. Our greatest need is for some kind of widespread spiritual change, and nothing that ignores this fact can provide lasting remedies for our problems either as individuals or as a society.

Where are we to turn for solutions, and what should we be looking for? One of the most difficult tests in life today is finding a sound spiritual and philosophical direction to follow. For many of us, this search is rather disorderly. In fact, we may not even recognize it as a process at all. It is more like wandering in a wilderness in which we hope to catch a glimpse of what we are looking for, whatever it may be. We grope because we lack a clear idea of what it is we seek. Maybe it's love, maybe security, maybe wholehearted acceptance, peace of mind, or a better sense of who we really are and what our purpose in life is. As we search, whether consciously or unconsciously, we find out more about what it is, and what it is not, that we are really looking for.

As we wander, we may become more aware of how lost we are, especially if we have tried a number of different paths that seemed promising for a while and then turned out to be dead ends. At least we are not alone: Many people are wandering and searching just like we are. But as it sinks in that we are not finding whatever it is that we are looking for, we may wish for some kind of guidance. If only there were a wise and selfless guide whom we could trust completely—someone who knows what we are looking for—someone to give us direction, encouragement, and spiritual sustenance. To such a person we would gladly give our heart.

Who, then, is this strong spiritual leader whom we await to guide us to the light of understanding and lead us out of the state in which humankind finds itself? We need a Spiritual Guide or Hero—a Messenger of God who can educate humanity in the ways that are needed.

There have been such Spiritual Guides in the past, among them Moses, Abraham, Krishna, Zoroaster, Jesus, and Muḥammad. Such figures have always appeared in the most benighted, depraved, reactionary, and corrupt parts of the known world. When such a Spiritual Guide appears, his chances of having a lasting effect on the world seem slight. Often he is poor to begin with; if not, he usually gives up his wealth in the interest of spiritual pursuits. He seldom has more than a rudimentary education, yet he astonishes people and alarms the powers that be with his all-encompassing knowledge and unsurpassed wisdom. He never accords with people's preconceived notions of a Messenger from God. Though he possesses miraculous abilities, he rarely uses them to persuade people to believe in him, preferring instead to touch human hearts with the example of his behavior and to enlighten their minds with his teachings. He seeks fellowship with all, most particularly with humble people of little means or low status and people who have been spurned by those who are more fortunate. He does not compromise the truth and curries favor with no one. Sadly, these qualities inevitably arouse the opposition of many who are jealous or afraid of change.

At first, only a handful of pure-hearted people recognize him, while political and religious leaders condemn him as a dangerous radical. Because his teachings often transcend those of the religious orthodoxy, he is denounced as an impostor or madman. As his reputation becomes known and spreads more widely, religious leaders begin to attack him with growing intensity.

Once he proclaims his identity and purpose, the Spiritual Guide is unrelenting in his determination to fulfill his responsibilities. He is bold and definite in his pronouncements. While he demands changes in people's conduct and social practices, he sets the example by demonstrating these changes in his own behavior. He brings teachings that are intended to help humanity well into the future—teachings that often differ radically from existing beliefs and practices. Not surprisingly, many individuals in positions of authority view the spread of his influence with dismay, for the new message and its bearer are seen as a threat to their positions of authority and their way of life.

The new Spiritual Guide persists in carrying out his mission despite unremitting persecution of himself and his followers. Amazingly, he forges ahead confidently, even when death seems imminent. He has a confidence and assurance that is not of this world. This fearlessness—this certitude, spiritual power, gentleness, and love—set him apart from everyone else because nobody has ever seen these qualities manifested in such a manner and to such a degree. He inspires awe and fear in many who meet him. A few people see in him a clear expression of the Divine Will of God.

Many centuries have passed since the Spiritual Guides of the past carried out their missions. Almost everything about them is open to question: What did they look like? Where and how did they live? How did they teach? While many people today still try to live by their teachings, scholars and theologians continue to debate what they actually taught.

Perhaps the most controversial questions revolve around the Spiritual Guide's relationship with God. Some people view him as God incarnate, while others accept him simply as a man of great courage and spiritual wisdom.

Other believers' views fall between the two extremes. The many differing views are a source of dissension between various sects claiming to follow the same Spiritual Guide. At times the dissension leads to violence and bloodshed, with each side claiming to have the one and only true understanding of the Spiritual Guide's teachings. As the factions bicker, fight, and compete with one another, they unwittingly drift away from the spiritual essence of his teachings. In the process, the spirit of the new religion is lost.

Despite the schisms that almost always break out following the death of a Spiritual Guide, his influence is always the cause of human progress. The progress resulting from Spiritual Guides who came in ancient times may no longer be discernable to those who are looking for a new infusion of divine guidance. Perhaps the Spiritual Guide came so long ago that it is practically impossible to appreciate the advances that were made, even though we benefit from them. Doctrinal feuding over the centuries, the theological imaginings that have been adopted as truth, and the general moral breakdown of society which precedes and continues for a time after the coming of another Spiritual Guide are other barriers. The spiritual springtime brought by the last Spiritual Guide has long since turned to summer, then autumn, and we have come back to the wintry spiritual conditions that prevailed at the time of his appearance.

We tend not to recognize the growth that has come about as a result of the influence of previous Spiritual Guides. Some of us go so far as to adopt the attitude that humans really have not advanced spiritually since they first appeared on earth.

However, this idea is quickly dispelled if we consider the state that we would be in if the Spiritual Guides had never appeared. Time after time, their influence has raised society to new levels of material and spiritual development. Through these Spiritual Guides humanity's conscience has been revived and further developed as the standards that they brought enabled people to distinguish between right and wrong and caused them to grow spiritually. Moses' Ten Commandments, which today represent what may seem like a very simple moral code, raised a large tribe from degradation and slavery to greatness and prominence. Buddha's Right Path brought about an unparalleled renaissance in the life of India and of other countries. The teachings of Jesus had an equally potent effect on the societies developing in Europe, Africa, and Asia. Muḥammad's message that there is only one merciful God not only united the warring tribes of Arabia but also provided the basis for a brilliant new society stretching from Spain to Indonesia in the Pacific, and it supplied the impetus for the European Renaissance. The Golden Rule, which all Spiritual Guides have taught, has led people to respect and love one another as they wish to be loved.

While it is true that most of us fall short of the high standards that have been set by the Spiritual Guides, the fact that we all know what the standards are and feel pangs of guilt when we fall short of them indicates the extent to which the Spiritual Guides have advanced the development of human morality.

The Spiritual Guides conquer hearts through love, truth, humility, and a spiritual strength that comes from God. Their example inspires people to develop virtues the Spiritual Guides manifest. Through them people discover their own spiritual capacity and learn how to grow spiritually.

It is clear that humanity today needs divine direction. Nothing else that we have devised is sufficient to resolve the many serious problems we face. But how would we recognize a new Spiritual Guide if one were to come? Where would he come from, and when? We may long for divine guidance, but we do not want to take a chance on being fooled, for there is no greater pain than that of disillusionment with a cause that we have believed in with our heart and soul. We may find it hard even to think about the possibility that a new Spiritual Guide might actually come. How would we know?

Recognizing a Spiritual Guide has never been easy. So much stands in the way of recognition: our prejudices, our fears, our preconceived notions of who or what a Spiritual Guide should look like, our reliance on well-meaning but misguided leaders. Tradition, superstition, and the desire for security are other barriers that, like a drawn blind, keep us from seeing the sunrise.

For whom do we wait? Some Jews anticipate a powerful warrior. Some Christians believe that Jesus will return on a cloud to raise the dead from their graves, lead the faithful to heaven, and destroy the earth. Some believe it will be easy to recognize Jesus upon his return by the nail holes in his hands. Certain Shiite Muslims expect the Twelfth Imam to finally emerge from the well in which they believe he has been hiding for the past eleven hundred years. According to this belief, once he returns, he will punish all who are not Shiites and will give the Muslim clergy absolute power over the world.

Followers of Zoroastrianism, Buddhism, and Hinduism cling to other traditions, all of them different. In India an ultramodern ashram called Auroville, which was led by a charismatic Hindu woman who called herself "the

Mother," seemed to many people to be the brightest hope for the future until it was torn apart by an internal power struggle.

Hundreds of other scenarios and schemes have been conceived, each with its own devoted following and each based on a particular set of understandings. Many people today are certain that they will recognize a new Spiritual Guide when he appears. However, the high priests of Jesus' day were certain that they understood the Messianic signs and knew what to look for, and still they did not recognize Jesus as a Spiritual Guide. Would we ourselves have recognized the spiritual leadership of a young Jewish carpenter from Nazareth who was born out of wedlock and associated with a prostitute? It has always been the case that when a new Spiritual Guide has appeared, those who were most certain that they would recognize him were blinded to the truth by their preconceptions.

So we continue to wait, our spiritual yearning unfulfilled, unsure of where to turn or whom to believe. In the marketplace of cures and ideas we see lots of competing philosophies and schemes that promise quick trips to spiritual paradise. Some people buy into the attractive offers, but many of us remain uncertain, wary of the rhetoric about instant salvation, wary of false prophets.

We may become angry—angry at ourselves for not having had the courage earlier to start our quest for something more satisfying to believe in than the lifestyle and the religion handed down by our parents. Deep down we may resent the years we have spent trying to accept something that has grown progressively difficult to accept.

What is religion all about anyway? Is it what we really think it is? We will consider these questions in the next chapter.

4

WHAT IS RELIGION ANYWAY?

Religion is not what most of us think it is. The word "religion" is derived from the Latin *religio,* which refers to the bond between man and the gods. It may also have been derived from Latin *religare,* meaning to bind back (*re-,* back + *ligare,* to bind, fasten). In its truest sense, religion should be more than a link between humanity and God. By teaching us how to draw closer to God, it should teach us how to draw closer to one another as well. Religion should be a source of unity, not division.

It is apparent that religion, as it is generally practiced, does not necessarily create strong bonds between diverse peoples. In fact, it has become terribly splintered: Christianity, Judaism, and Islam have all experienced divisions within their faiths, not to mention the existence of thousands of other less well-known organized religious systems. None of these divisions were created by the Spiritual Guides around whom they are centered.

What would Jesus do if he were to appear today and survey the institutions that profess a belief in him? What would Moses and Muḥammad think of the way their teachings are now being practiced? How would Buddha, who opposed idol worship, feel if he were to see people genuflecting before massive gold statues of himself?

Religion is in trouble. Many religious leaders can see this, even though they are loath to admit it. We are attempting to stretch the teachings of ancient Spiritual Guides to fit today's needs. Despite valiant efforts, it simply is not working. And new approaches based on the latest social philosophies, which are sometimes adopted by the clergy, are not working either. We might ask if, by doing this, the clergies are admitting that the Spiritual Guides from whom their religions spring did not provide guidance for many of today's problems.

Perhaps an answer to that question could be found by asking other questions: Is it possible that the Spiritual Guides of the past never intended to provide solutions to all problems for all time? Is it possible that God's guidance for humankind is revealed in progressive stages that take into consideration humanity's relative level of maturity at the time? The process of evolution applies to all living things—why not to religion and spiritual development as well?

Religion can be likened to a school in which humanity is the student body and God is the principal. God creates the curriculum and selects the teachers—the Spiritual Guides, or Divine Educators. Principles of spiritual development and social awareness are taught in every grade by these Spiritual Guides. The teachings in each grade build on those of the previous one, taking into account the students' level of maturity and their readiness to advance. You would not teach calculus to four year olds or five year olds. A foundation in basic principles of mathematics must be built first. Wouldn't a wise and compassionate principal educate in the same way?

The Spiritual Guides can be seen as teachers, or Divine Educators, of whom there are many. Though they all have different names and have come to different places at different times in history, they have all had essentially the same mission: to prepare their students to go on to the next grade. Each Divine Educator reviews the teachings of his predecessors, making sure his students properly understand the fundamental spiritual lessons upon which he must build. The light he shines on the past cuts through the dust of dogma and theology, exposing the true identity and purpose of previous Divine Educators and strengthening the foundation of religion. He establishes a new set of values and spiritual practices that is designed to meet the needs of a new age. He inspires in his followers a renewed love for God and teaches them the importance of developing their spiritual faculties, showing them how to do it. He provides guidance for creating a just and spiritual society and promises that others like himself will come in the future, continuing the process of divine education through which God's will for humanity is progressively revealed. This is a never-ending process.

Most people are not yet aware of this process, just as most people in the time of Columbus were not aware that the world was round. Yet the process of education—of the progressive revelation of God's will for humanity—goes on as it always has and always will. It is a fundamental spiritual law of life.

Humanity has largely ignored or remained unaware of this law, choosing instead to continue following one Divine Educator or another instead of going on to the next spiritual grade. We have tended either to become fanatically attached to the Spiritual Guide our forefathers revered or to become indifferent toward him, rejecting him as irrelevant.

It seems reasonable to assume that God is practical, among other things. Thus it would not have made sense for Him to direct Moses to teach the Hebrews that men and women were equal at that time. Certainly, God knows that men and women have been and always will be equal, but this is an idea that people were not ready to accept four thousand years ago. It was difficult enough for them to grasp the concept of the oneness of God. In time, as humanity matured, the principle of the equality of the sexes would be a part of the teachings of a future Spiritual Guide.

Consider the state of the world in Jesus' day. What were people's perceptions of reality? For most, their hamlet or town was the center of the universe. Among the Roman elite, the world was thought to consist of little more than their empire. Had someone attempted to tell the people living two thousand years ago that there would someday be airplanes, computers, robotics, television, or that human beings would one day walk on the moon, that person would have been branded a lunatic. Although more and more of us are recognizing the need for harmony and unity among the nations of the world, the people of Jesus' time were not even able to conceive such a possibility. At the time, the planet was largely uncharted. Natural barriers—mighty mountain ranges, oceans, and seas—kept people apart. The people of North America were not aware of the people in Israel, and the Israelites were not aware of the Native Americans. Hundreds of other tribes and peoples never knew of one another's existence. It would have been futile to call for peace and harmony among the nations. Humanity was not yet ready for it. But one day the time would be right, and in that day, a Spiritual Guide would not only call for its development but would also reveal a divine plan to implement it.

Does this concept of religion as an evolutionary process make sense? Some of us will find it easy to embrace. Others may be skeptical, finding it difficult to accept because it seems too simple. Or perhaps we see the Spiritual Guide whom we have been taught to follow as spiritually unique and superior to all of the other Divine Educators, making it difficult for us to accept the others.

But many Spiritual Guides have appeared, and a fresh measure of divine truth has been released into the world through each. Elaborate attempts have been made to refute each new revelation, including military campaigns intended to squelch what some condemned as the machinations of the devil. For example, the holy crusades of the Christians were intended to wrest the Holy Land from the Muslims and crush Islam. However, when religion resorts to the sword to promote its interests and vanquish its foes, it loses its spiritual authenticity.

Over time, God has sent Abraham, Krishna, Moses, Buddha, Zoroaster, Jesus, Muḥammad, and others to enlighten humankind, and no earthly force, however powerful, has been able to keep these Divine Educators, these

Spiritual Guides, from carrying out their missions.

The Divine Educators are unique in the grand phenomenon of life. They represent a special level of creation. None of history's great philosophers and statesmen can compare with them, not even such greats as Aristotle, Plato, Tolstoy, Tagore, or Gandhi. The Divine Educators are not simply people who happen to possess outstanding spiritual capacities. They are a link between God and humanity, divinely chosen individuals who serve as a channel conveying God's will for humanity. In a sense, to know them is to know God, but this does not mean that they are God. They are, however, the closest we can get to Him. God is an unknowable essence. No one, no matter how holy, can ever know Him directly. Whatever picture of Him we may imagine is an illusion, for creation cannot know the mind of its Creator.

The Divine Educator is a special being of a higher order. Because of this, it is impossible for us to comprehend his nature. To understand this better, consider the various levels of being in creation. Though all levels of life have certain things in common, there are fundamental differences. The lower levels simply cannot appreciate the world of the higher levels. Can a lily understand a bird? Can a dog truly comprehend a human being? Can we really know the nature of a Divine Educator? No, but we can feel his impact, whether we accept him or not. He does things no one else can do. Because of him great masses of people change their attitudes and behavior and grow spiritually. His presence and his revelation of God's will set in motion the formation of a new civilization and bring about changes in virtually all phases of life. It is no mere coincidence that such changes occur. The process has occurred too many times for it to be explained away as mere coincidence. The Christian, Muslim, Hebrew, Hindu, and Buddhist civilizations did not spring into being by accident.

There is no special physical characteristic that makes the Divine Educator stand out. Outwardly, he looks like any other human being. This can be a stumbling block for those who expect God's spokesman to be physically different than any mere human. He resembles us and is even susceptible to the same bodily imperfections as we are. For instance, Moses is believed to have been a stutterer. Unlike us, however, the Divine Educator has completely surrendered his will to God's, manifesting only God's will. Once chosen, he no longer makes choices based on his own desires. Doing God's will is his only desire, his reason for living, even though it means enduring constant hardship and even death.

The role of the Divine Educator in our relationship with God is absolutely essential. Without him we would be guided by nothing but our own fantasies. We would be like a crew on a captainless ship.

To describe how God communicates with humanity through the Divine Educators requires a metaphor. Think of God as the sun and the Divine Educator as a mirror that faces the sun. When we look into the mirror we can see the sun's light. If we are close enough to the mirror, we can feel the sun's heat. Just as the mirror reflects the sun, the Divine Educator reflects the qualities of God. In that sense, when we turn to the Divine Educator, we turn to God.

Historically, people have always had difficulty understanding the Divine Educator's relationship with God. Yet they are touched by him and by his tremendous love and wisdom. Logic and analysis usually have nothing to do with their decision to accept him. It is usually a matter of the heart.

There are two sides to the Divine Educator: the human and the divine. The human side is distinctive because each Divine Educator is a unique individual. Like every human being, he has a childhood and playmates. He has likes and dislikes, experiences joy and sorrow, laughs and cries. He feels pain when he is injured. He knows, too, the smells of the stable and of the street. Historical accounts have established that Jesus was a carpenter and that his friends were fishermen; Moses is known to have killed a man; Muḥammad was an illiterate camel driver. Some of the Divine Educators married and had children.

However, when we look at all of the Divine Educators from a spiritual point of view, they are essentially the same. They are all the repositories of the Holy Spirit. To better understand the difference between the two sides of the Divine Educator, think of him as a lighted lamp. The lamp represents his human form; the light represents the Holy Spirit. Although the light may radiate from different lamps, we always recognize it as the light, regardless of the lamp from which it radiates. From whatever source it radiates, we always recognize the light as light.

The Divine Educator not only sheds spiritual light on the present and future, providing for our spiritual and social needs, but also casts a bright, steady light on the past. Elaborating on the past enables us to properly understand and appreciate his directions for the present and future; without this elaboration, our deeply entrenched, misguided notions and prejudices would keep us from understanding his message. He clarifies the identity and true purpose of his predecessors, cutting through layers of dogma that obscure the truth. Jesus, for example, said that if the people to whom he came had really known and understood Moses, they would have known and, therefore, recognized Jesus.

Even those who sincerely accept the Divine Educator can unwittingly betray his purpose. For example, if we become overly enamored of the lamp and embrace it with such vigor that we block out the light of reason and intelligence, fanaticism follows.

Though the spiritual essence of the Divine Educators is the same, their revelations differ according to the level of maturity and the capacity of the people to whom they came. As humanity has matured, more spiritual light has been cast with each successive revelation.

Through the efforts of the Divine Educators humanity's moral consciousness has developed and evolved. This is a never-ending process, for there will always be room for growth and spiritual development. Each successive Divine Educator has been the cause of a new stage of growth and development. Through Moses humanity gained an appreciation for spiritual law, a feel for monotheism. Through Jesus humanity gained an understanding of the meaning of love and how to demonstrate it, and the value of sacrifice. Muḥammad taught the value of submitting one's will to God and the importance of courtesy and kindness. Buddha taught us lessons about compassion and service to others.

Today our planet yearns for a fresh measure of the light of God. Mercifully, this need has not gone unnoticed. Millions of people around the world believe that a new Divine Educator has come. They believe that every spot on earth is now illumined. For those who have come to know about this Divine Educator, their wait is finally over; their search has come to a happy conclusion. The following three chapters tell the story of this new message from God and the circumstances of its revelation. Those who are aware of this new revelation see it as the fulfillment of God's ancient promise that He will never abandon us and that we will always have a Spiritual Guide to help us draw closer to Him. They believe that the Promised One for our time has indeed come.

5
THE GATE

The account you are about to read is not a fairy tale—it really happened. You might think that such a momentous series of events would deserve a global announcement that would bring it to everyone's attention. But when these events occurred in the mid-1800s only a few people appreciated what was taking place, and only with the passage of time will their full significance be truly understood. Even today those who know the story cannot grasp its full significance. Hundreds of years from now, when the events are carefully sorted out and their ultimate impact is evident, humanity will have a much clearer picture of what really happened. They will be astonished that more people did not realize that someone had brought the desperately needed solution to humanity's problems.

On 24 May 1844 the American inventor Samuel F. B. Morse sent the first long-distance message by telegraph, an instrument that would revolutionize communications around the world. The message he tapped out in his Baltimore office was received almost instantaneously in Washington, D.C. It read, "What hath God wrought!"

The day before, halfway around the world in the ancient city of Shiraz, Persia (now Iran), an even more dramatic event had taken place between two people in a modest house. Though Morse was not aware of what had happened in Shiraz, his telegraph message was so fitting that in the future it will always be associated with that momentous event.

This was a time of great messianic expectation in many parts of the world. Sincere believers of many different traditions were turning to the scriptures of their respective religions and finding prophecies that they believed indicated some great change was about to take place in the world. In Europe and North America many found evidence in the Christian scriptures to support the belief that the return of Jesus was imminent. In the Middle East, an uncannily similar process was taking place in relation to various prophecies of the Koran and certain Islamic traditions.

A devout young Muslim named Mullá Ḥusayn was on a special quest. He belonged to a religious order whose members believed that God would send a long-awaited Promised One who would fulfill certain Islamic prophecies and would appear in or near Persia in the year 1844.

5 – THE GATE

In his heart Mullá Ḥusayn felt certain that the Promised One was alive, and he was determined to find him. He felt compelled to travel north from his native home in southwestern Persia to Shiraz and set out with his brother and nephew for that city. It was as if some mysterious force were drawing him to the north.

When the three men reached the gates of Shiraz, Mullá Ḥusayn suggested that his companions go on ahead to a nearby mosque, where he intended to join them later for the evening prayer. Something was attracting his heart to the city.

While walking outside the city gates a few hours before sunset, Mullá Ḥusayn noticed the radiant face of a young man wearing a green turban. The color of his turban signified that he was a descendant of Muḥammad, the prophet and founder of Islam. Mullá Ḥusayn stood spellbound as the smiling young man approached and greeted him, embracing him warmly as if he were a long lost friend. When this magnetic young man invited him to visit his home, Mullá Ḥusayn found himself unable to resist the invitation even though he felt he should be joining his companions at the mosque.

Apart from the host, no one in that city, not even Mullá Ḥusayn, knew what was about to take place in that house. The young host seemed strangely familiar to Mullá Ḥusayn, though the two had never met before. The host had water brought so that Mullá Ḥusayn could wash off the dust from his long journey. He insisted on pouring the water over Mullá Ḥusayn's hands himself. Then a refreshing drink was served, and this was followed by tea, which the host himself prepared and served. After the customary evening prayer, the two began to talk.

Without provocation the host spontaneously asked Mullá Ḥusayn about his search, inquiring about the qualities of the person he sought. Mullá Ḥusayn began to explain: The Promised One for whom he was searching would be a descendent of Muḥammad, in his twenties, possessed of innate knowledge, and would abstain from smoking and be free from physical ailments.

After pausing awhile, the host said to Mullá Ḥusayn, "Behold, all these signs are manifest in Me!"[1] He then proceeded to demonstrate how he fulfilled each of the requirements. When Mullá Ḥusayn had started out on his quest, he had privately decided on two additional requirements that the Promised One must fulfill: The first was to explain a number of mysterious passages in a book that Mullá Ḥusayn had written. This the host did after only briefly glancing at a few passages of the book. Furthermore, the host went on to explain other truths that Mullá Ḥusayn had never heard before. After this, to Mullá Ḥusayn's great astonishment, the host rapidly and spontaneously began to write an interpretation of one of the more obscure chapters of the Koran. This was the second requirement Mullá Ḥusayn had privately devised to test anyone who claimed to be the Promised One; however, the host had fulfilled the requirement before Mullá Ḥusayn even had the chance to ask him for the commentary.

As the hours passed it struck Mullá Ḥusayn that the young man sitting before him was unlike anyone else in the world. The words that streamed from his lips and his pen went far beyond mere eloquence—they could not have been produced by any ordinary man. They could only be a divine revelation from one who was the Voice of God.

By dawn, after many hours of prayer and discussion, Mullá Ḥusayn knew that he had finally found the object of his long quest—that this young host was the Promised One who fulfilled the prophecies he had studied and prayed about so earnestly. His name was 'Alí-Muḥammad, known today as "the Báb," meaning "the Gate" in Arabic.

"'This Revelation, so suddenly and impetuously thrust upon me,'" Mullá Ḥusayn later wrote,

> "came as a thunderbolt which, for a time, seemed to have benumbed my faculties. I was blinded by its dazzling splendour and overwhelmed by its crushing force. Excitement, joy, awe, and wonder stirred the depths of my soul. Predominant among these emotions was a sense of gladness and strength which seemed to have transfigured me. How feeble and impotent, how dejected and timid, I had felt previously! Then I could neither write nor walk, so tremulous were my hands and feet. Now, however, the knowledge of His Revelation had galvanised my being."[2]

The Báb told Mullá Ḥusayn that seventeen other individuals from all parts of Persia must, alone and unaided, spontaneously seek the Promised One and recognize the Báb's claim. Mullá Ḥusayn and these individuals would be appointed as his chosen disciples. Miraculously, after forty days had elapsed seventeen souls arose one by one and recognized the Báb as the Promised One they had been awaiting. Illumination came to them in a variety of ways: through dreams, fasting, prayer, and visions. Among these disciples was a distinguished woman called Ṭáhirih, who was a brilliant scholar and poet. Stirred by the Báb's teachings, she became an illustrious heroine in the cause of women's rights. Sadly, she was later killed for her belief in the Báb and in those rights, but she is remembered today as one of the greatest heroines of the Bahá'í Faith.

The Báb had special instructions for each of the disciples. Many of them, including Mullá Ḥusayn, took to the road, traveling throughout Persia to share the Báb's message with the people. Mullá Ḥusayn was instructed to travel to Tehran, the capital of Persia. The Báb told him that some great mystery was enshrined in that city—a mystery that would transcend in its greatness even the spiritual light shed by Hijaz (the birthplace of Muḥammad) and Shiraz (the birthplace of the Báb).

The message spread rapidly as the disciples traveled far and wide. As has always been the case whenever someone claims to have a new revelation from God, those who were in positions of power and influence that might be threatened by the teachings that the Báb brought opposed the new religion immediately. Members of the clergy as well as the government began to wage a pogrom to stamp out the fledgling movement, accusing the Báb and his followers of heresy against Islam.

As the spiritual blaze ignited by the Báb and his teachings grew in intensity, so did the violence of the controversy it provoked and the resulting persecution of his followers. A number of the disciples were arrested and tortured, and one died while in prison. Peace and security all around the country were threatened by the storm of controversy the movement was setting off. Alarmed by the upheaval in his province, the governor of Shiraz had the Báb arrested and severely punished.

However, nothing the clergy organized was able to stop the Báb's message from spreading like wildfire. When it started attracting the merchant class and even some members of the clergy, the shah could no longer afford to ignore the commotion. He decided to send a trusted and knowledgeable advisor to investigate the movement, which was showing no sign of receding. He commissioned a scholar named Vaḥíd—reputed to be the most erudite, eloquent, and influential of his subjects—to interview the Báb and learn the real nature of this movement. The shah completely trusted Vaḥíd because of his impartiality, his broadmindedness, and his profound spiritual insight.

When Vaḥíd met with the Báb he was astounded by the originality of the young man's mind and his insight into the most complicated spiritual matters. The Báb even answered difficult and important questions that Vaḥíd had meant to ask but had forgotten to bring up, and he did so with amazing succinctness and clarity. After three sessions with the Báb, Vaḥíd was convinced beyond any doubt that the one before him drew his knowledge from a realm to which he himself had no access. He accepted the Báb wholeheartedly, later telling friends that in the presence of the Báb he felt himself to be as "'lowly as the dust beneath His feet.'"[3] So firmly was he convinced of the Báb's claims that five years later Vaḥíd died defending his belief.

Other noted scholars accepted the Báb's message as well, as did a number of government officials and religious leaders. Word of the Báb's extraordinary qualities and powers passed swiftly from city to city, from village to village. Crowds of people flocked to places where he was known to be, many seeking to be healed, others just hoping to catch a glimpse of this person who claimed to be the Promised One.

The shah's court was becoming extremely disturbed because the unrest in the country was seriously challenging the established order. The shah felt it necessary to summon the Báb to the capital. However, the prime minister, Ḥájí Mírzá Áqásí, was afraid that the Báb might influence the shah. If this were to happen it would seriously threaten his own position as prime minister. He persuaded the shah to change his mind and instead send the Báb to prison in the barren mountains of Azerbaijan in the northwest part of Persia. This, he thought, would stamp out the Báb's influence and render him powerless in short order.

Though the Báb was now a prisoner, he knew he still had much to do. Though denied even a lamp to light his cell at night, he wrote voluminously. Besides producing commentaries on the Koran, he composed prayers, homilies, orations, scientific treatises, doctrinal dissertations, and laws and ordinances for the consolidation of the new religion and the direction of its activities. He also wrote epistles to the religious authorities of every city in Persia, pointing out to them where they had erred. Amazingly, the epistles managed to reach their destinations. He also revealed a book of laws and precepts called the Bayán. This important work decreed many religious reforms and annulled some of the religious and social practices of Christianity and Islam while upholding the legitimacy of the revelations of both Jesus and Muḥammad. The Báb proclaimed that a new day had dawned and new practices were needed. He wrote, "Verily I say, immensely exalted is this Day above the days of the Apostles of old."[4]

In the Bayán, the Báb explains that the major purpose of his mission was to herald and pave the way for the coming of another Divine Educator, one who would set in motion and be the driving force of an even mightier revelation from God. This new revelation, he claimed, would spiritualize and unite the entire human race. He referred to this Divine

Educator as "Him Whom God shall make manifest"[5] and explained that his coming was imminent—that all should turn to this new faith.

Although the Báb spent five years in prison, this did not deter his followers from practicing or teaching their beliefs. Believers streamed from all over the country, hoping to visit the Báb in prison or merely to catch a glimpse of his face from his prison cell. The enthusiasm with which they continued to share the Báb's message was so great that the government and the ecclesiastical hierarchy stiffened their resolve to wipe out the upstart religion.

Their most effective instrument against the followers of the Báb was to be the mass of the people, the vast majority of whom were illiterate and therefore dependent on the clergy for guidance. They could easily be incited to action, stirred into a frenzied state in which they were capable of tearing to pieces anyone whom they perceived as an infidel.

Not only did the Muslim clergy use their pulpits to denounce the Báb as a heretic and a sorcerer, but they also sanctioned and often led murderous assaults against his followers. Appallingly grim and barbarous tortures were inflicted upon the Báb's followers. Some were shot from cannons, others were decapitated, dragged through the streets, stoned to death, or subjected to other heinous tortures. Not even children or elderly women were spared from the wrath of these mobs. So bestial was the onslaught that European eyewitnesses living in Persia at the time wrote home aghast at what they had seen. Their shocking accounts were published in the press.

Altogether, tens of thousands of followers of the Báb were martyred for their beliefs, many others were maimed for life, and still others were imprisoned and tortured. Damage to their property was extensive. The bloodbath turned brother against brother and father against son.

News of the massacre and torture of the Báb's followers eventually reached him in prison. Overcome by sorrow, he wept for days on end, refusing all food and drink. For six months he did not pick up his pen to write.

In 1848 the prime minister ordered that the Báb be taken to Tabríz, the capital of the province where he was imprisoned, for examination. The Báb knew that a fraudulent trial awaited him there. However, this occasion afforded him the opportunity to proclaim his revelation formally in a public arena. Before the governor of Azerbaijan as well as the heir to the shah's throne and all of the assembled government and religious dignitaries, he proclaimed,

> I am, I am the Promised One! I am the One Whose name you have for a thousand years invoked, at Whose mention you have risen,

> Whose advent you have longed to witness, and the hour of Whose Revelation you have prayed to God to hasten. Verily, I say, it is incumbent upon the peoples of both the East and the West to obey My word, and to pledge allegiance to My person.[6]

The consequences of this bold proclamation were inevitable: The Báb was sentenced to death.

The date of his execution by firing squad was set for 9 July 1850. It was to be a spectacular event, designed by the authorities to show the citizenry who really held the power in Persia. Some ten thousand people gathered around the site of the execution to witness the demise of this figure who had set off such a storm of passions in their country.

In the cell in Tabríz that served as his final prison, the Báb was talking confidentially to his secretary when an attendant arrived to fetch him and lead him to his execution. The Báb turned to the attendant and said sternly, "Not until I have said to him all those things that I wish to say can any earthly power silence Me. Though all the world be armed against Me, yet shall it be powerless to deter Me from fulfilling, to the last word, My intention."[7]

The colonel of the regiment that had been ordered to carry out the execution begged to be released from this duty, fearing that it would provoke the wrath of God. The Báb offered his assurance, saying, "Follow your instructions, and if your intention be sincere, the Almighty is surely able to relieve you of your perplexity."[8]

The Báb and a youth who had begged for the privilege of sacrificing his life with him were suspended by ropes from a spike driven into a pillar in the prison square. There they faced a firing squad of 750 soldiers arranged in three rows of 250 men each.

When the colonel gave the command to fire, each row in turn opened fire until all of the soldiers had discharged their rifles. When the smoke from the guns cleared, the spectators could barely believe their eyes. The Báb was nowhere in sight, and the youth who had been at his side was standing alive and unhurt before them. The volley of shots had merely severed the ropes that had held them.

A frantic search followed. The Báb was found in his cell, uninjured and unperturbed, finishing his interrupted conversation with his secretary. As the attendant approached again, the Báb said, "I have finished My conversation. . . . Now you may proceed to fulfill your intention."[9]

The attendant was so unnerved that he left the scene and resigned from his post. The colonel refused to allow his squad to participate in any further attempts to harm the Báb and ordered his men to leave the prison immediately. However, others readily volunteered to replace those who had left.

Once again the Báb and his companion were suspended by ropes before the firing squad. But before the order to fire was issued, the Báb addressed the thousands of onlookers with these final words: "'O wayward generation! Had you believed in Me every one of you would have followed the example of this youth, who stood in rank above most of you, and would have willingly sacrificed himself in My path. The day will come when you will have recognized Me; that day I shall have ceased to be with you.'"[10] On this second attempt the bullets tore into the bodies of the thirty-one-year-old prophet and his young companion. While the bullets all but destroyed their bodies, the faces of the Báb and his young companion remained virtually unmarred.

As the shots were fired, a violent gale swept over Tabríz, setting off a blinding dust storm that left the city in darkness from noon until evening.

This devastating loss of their beloved leader plunged the followers of the Báb—known as Bábís—into deep sorrow. Without the Báb's guidance, some felt utterly incapable of moving forward. But the faithful held on to the primary purpose of the teachings of the Báb:

to prepare for the coming of "Him Whom God shall make manifest," the Divine Educator who would spiritualize and unite the entire human race. In his writings the Báb revealed the name of this individual: "Well is it with him who fixeth his gaze upon the Order of *Bahá'u'lláh,* and rendereth thanks unto his Lord. For He will assuredly be made manifest."[11] In fact, this tragic loss did not squelch the Bábí movement as members of the clergy and the government had hoped it would; it only served to deepen the devotion and faith of its adherents.

A young nobleman from Tehran who was known by the title "Bahá'u'lláh," meaning "the Glory of God" in Arabic, was one of the Báb's most ardent followers. Tehran was the city that the Báb had said was spiritually of even greater significance than Hijaz or Shiraz. In fact, the sole reason that Mullá Ḥusayn had traveled to Tehran at the Báb's behest was to deliver a message from the Báb to this young nobleman. From that point onward the Báb and Bahá'u'lláh had carried on a steady correspondence. It was to Bahá'u'lláh whom the Báb had sent his pen case, his seal rings, and documents shortly before his execution.

The Báb had prepared a number of his disciples to expect the appearance of "Him Whom God shall make manifest" in their lifetimes. In fact, he said, some of them would even meet him face-to-face.

6
THE GLORY OF GOD

The Persian authorities were relieved after the Báb's execution, thinking that the source of the tumult in their land for the past six years was eliminated. They believed the Bábí movement would not last long, and soon normality would return. There was evidence to support this assessment because the Bábís were in a state of disarray. Though their faith remained strong, the continued assault on their community had decimated their numbers and had left them terribly demoralized.

The Bábís continued to suffer. Not only were they harassed and hunted down by the authorities, but there were also internal problems. Without a leader the new faith began to splinter as the believers feverishly sought the one whom the Báb had promised would emerge to guide them, the one he had alluded to as "Him Whom God shall make manifest." A number of misled individuals proclaimed that they were the Báb's successor, adding to the confusion and disarray.

Some of the Bábís grew frustrated. There was an impulse to avenge the slaying of the Báb and the brutal treatment of their fellow believers, even though the Báb had prohibited the practice of seeking vengeance. In the summer of 1852, despite the pleas of their fellow believers, two grief-stricken young men devised a plot to assassinate the shah. Their poorly conceived plan failed, leaving the shah with only minor injuries and setting off a storm of persecution against the Bábís.

The government's reaction was predictably brutal. The authorities struck out in every direction at the Bábí community, stepping up the persecution and slaughter of its adherents. As part of the pogrom, those who were known to be Bábí leaders were targeted for a greater measure of persecution and were rounded up and arrested. One of these figures was the young nobleman known by the title "Bahá'u'lláh," meaning "the Glory of God."

Bahá'u'lláh was no ordinary man. Born on 12 November 1817 to a wealthy family that traced its ancestry to the pre-Islamic monarchy of Persia, he was the son of a well-known minister in the shah's court. Though Bahá'u'lláh had grown up accustomed to material comfort, wealth, and privilege, these things held no interest for him. His childhood had been marked by a gentle and kind disposition, his youth by both immense generosity and knowledge, though his formal schooling was minimal. By the time he reached adulthood he was known as "Father of the Poor" for his extraordinary acts of kindness and generosity to the downtrodden in the streets of Tehran, and he was highly respected for his uncanny knowledge and wisdom. It was Bahá'u'lláh whom the Báb had sent Mullá Ḥusayn to find in Tehran, and Bahá'u'lláh had arisen immediately afterward to consecrate his life to vigorously and fearlessly spreading the Báb's message. Thus it was Bahá'u'lláh to whom many of the Bábís turned as a natural leader after the Báb's execution.

Because of this position of prominence among the Bábís, it was assumed that Bahá'u'lláh was somehow involved in plotting the attempt on the life of the shah. Bahá'u'lláh was arrested in Tehran, bound in chains, and marched barefoot and bareheaded under the blistering sun to the dreaded "Black Pit," an underground dungeon near the shah's palace. Angry onlookers stripped Bahá'u'lláh of his outer garments, jeered at him, and pelted him with stones.

When Bahá'u'lláh reached the Black Pit, he was led through a pitch-black corridor and down three steep flights of stairs to his place of confinement. Not a ray of light penetrated the thick stone walls. Nearly 150 other prisoners were there—many of them Bábís, but also thieves, assassins, and highwaymen—all of them chained together. Most of the prisoners had neither clothes nor bedding to lie on. The floor was damp, layered with filth, and crawling with vermin. The stench was almost unbearable. Bahá'u'lláh's feet were placed in stocks, and a chain so heavy that it cut into his flesh was fastened around his neck. He was chained to five other Bábís.

It was in this seemingly hopeless situation that Bahá'u'lláh felt "the first stirrings of God's Revelation within His soul."[1] In a dream one night, a voice directed the following words at him:

> "Verily, We shall render Thee victorious by Thyself and by Thy Pen. Grieve Thou not for that which hath befallen Thee, neither be Thou afraid, for Thou art in safety. Erelong will God raise up the treasures of the earth—men who will aid Thee through Thyself and through Thy Name, wherewith God hath revived the hearts of such as have recognized Him."[2]

Divine enlightenment came to Bahá'u'lláh while he was in the Black Pit, charging his soul with an energy he had never experienced before:

> . . . though the galling weight of the chains and the stench-filled air allowed Me but little sleep, still in those infrequent moments of

> slumber I felt as if something flowed from the crown of My head over My breast, even as a mighty torrent that precipitateth itself upon the earth from the summit of a lofty mountain. Every limb of My body would, as a result, be set afire. At such moments My tongue recited what no man could bear to hear.[3]

This revelation came to Bahá'u'lláh in the form of a heavenly Maiden who appeared to him in a dream, just as the Holy Spirit had descended on Jesus in the form of the Dove and as it had made itself known to Moses through the Burning Bush. Bahá'u'lláh later wrote,

> "While engulfed in tribulations I heard a most wondrous, a most sweet voice, calling above My head. Turning My face, I beheld a Maiden—the embodiment of the remembrance of the name of My Lord—suspended in the air before Me. So rejoiced was she in her very soul that her countenance shone with the ornament of the good-pleasure of God, and her cheeks glowed with the brightness of the All-Merciful. Betwixt earth and heaven she was raising a call which captivated the hearts and minds of men. She was imparting to both My inward and outer being tidings which rejoiced My soul, and the

> souls of God's honored servants. Pointing with her finger unto My head, she addressed all who are in heaven and all who are on earth, saying: 'By God! This is the Best-Beloved of the worlds, and yet ye comprehend not. This is the Beauty of God amongst you, and the power of His sovereignty within you, could ye but understand. This is the Mystery of God and His Treasure, the Cause of God and His glory unto all who are in the kingdoms of Revelation and of creation, if ye be of them that perceive.'"[4]

This account, which is written in Bahá'u'lláh's own hand, is unique in religious history. It is the only firsthand description of the experience of divine revelation.

Bahá'u'lláh's mission was to unify humanity—to bring all people closer to God and closer to one another. It was not enough that we had our disparate nations and races. Now was the time, with the message brought by Bahá'u'lláh from God, for humanity to set aside its differences and unite. As Bahá'u'lláh writes, "It is incumbent upon all the peoples of the world to reconcile their differences, and, with perfect unity and peace, abide beneath the shadow of the Tree of His care and loving-kindness. . . . Soon will the present-day order be rolled up, and a new one spread out in its stead."[5]

6– THE GLORY OF GOD

For four months Bahá'u'lláh was held in the Black Pit, suffering in unimaginable ways. There were some who wanted to keep him there until he died, but he was cleared of all charges, and the government had no choice but to release him. Though Bahá'u'lláh was released and was, in a sense, free, his life would never again be as carefree as it had been. The Russian consul to Persia, who admired Bahá'u'lláh deeply, had managed to persuade the Persian authorities to release him, but Bahá'u'lláh could not stay in Tehran, nor even in his native land, for he was now an exile. He was given a month to leave the country.

The Russian consul offered Bahá'u'lláh refuge in Russia, where he could live in safety, but Bahá'u'lláh politely declined the offer, deciding instead to leave for Baghdad, Iraq, which was still at that time a province of the Ottoman Empire. Still suffering from the physical effects of spending four months in the dungeon, Bahá'u'lláh, with his family and a few friends, began a three-month journey to Iraq in the middle of an exceptionally severe winter. Snow in the mountain passes slowed travel, and the cold brought further hardship for the ill-clad travelers, whose party included a number of small children and frail elderly. In some ways, Bahá'u'lláh's banishment from his native land recalled Abraham's expulsion from Ur, Moses' exodus from Egypt, and Muḥammad's flight from Mecca.

In April 1853 Bahá'u'lláh and his party finally reached Baghdad. Though none of the residents of Baghdad knew who he really was when he arrived, Bahá'u'lláh quickly became a center of attraction. People sensed that there was something special about him. Many expressed puzzlement at the fact that he was not a prince, or a cleric, or a noted scholar. They wondered who this illustrious figure could be. All sorts of people—princes and peasants, clergy and laymen, Arabs, Kurds, Persians, government officials—streamed to his home seeking spiritual illumination.

However, the first year in Baghdad was full of great difficulty for Bahá'u'lláh. A younger half-brother named Mírzá Yaḥyá burned with jealousy at all of the attention Bahá'u'lláh was receiving and conspired against him. He and a small band of supporters stirred up trouble among the Bábís, spreading malicious rumors about Bahá'u'lláh. Even though Bahá'u'lláh never sought a leadership role, people were drawn to him to seek his advice and counsel. Witnessing this day after day almost drove the half-brother to distraction. His efforts to spread rumors about Bahá'u'lláh created divisions, suspicion, and bitterness where there otherwise would have been none.

Feeling that his presence was becoming a source of discord and sorrow and not wanting to hurt anyone's feelings, Bahá'u'lláh withdrew from Baghdad and headed for a remote area in the mountains of Kurdistan to live in solitude. He hoped that his departure would end the dissension among the Báb's followers. During those days of seclusion, Bahá'u'lláh lived very simply, at times seeking shelter in a cave. He often chanted the praises of God, recalled in tears the plight of Jesus and Muḥammad, and sang the praises of that Maiden who personified the Spirit of God within him. This period of seclusion and withdrawal parallels the path taken by every other Divine Educator before him.

Bahá'u'lláh writes of this time:

> In the early days of Our arrival in this land, when We discerned the signs of impending events, We decided, ere they happened, to retire. We betook Ourselves to the wilderness, and there, separated and alone, led for two years a life of complete solitude. From Our eyes there rained tears of anguish, and in Our bleeding heart there surged an ocean of agonizing pain. Many a night We had no food for sustenance, and many a day Our body found no rest. By Him Who hath My being between His hands! notwithstanding

> these showers of afflictions and unceasing calamities, Our soul was wrapt in blissful joy, and Our whole being evinced an ineffable gladness. For in Our solitude We were unaware of the harm or benefit, the health or ailment, of any soul. Alone, We communed with Our spirit, oblivious of the world and all that is therein.[6]

Bahá'u'lláh remained in the wilderness of Kurdistan content to be alone in his communion with God indefinitely.

After two years of removal from the world and its obligations, however, Bahá'u'lláh knew that soon he had to return to Baghdad to revive the ailing Bábí community. Though he knew that returning would bring an end to the peace and tranquillity he had come to treasure while living in this remote place, he knew that it was the will of God for him to return.

Sadly, the bickering and dissension among the Bábís in Baghdad had grown worse in the absence of Bahá'u'lláh's leadership. The state of the Bábís in Persia had also worsened. When some of the Bábís discovered where Bahá'u'lláh was and begged for him to return, he reluctantly agreed to their request. In March of 1856 Bahá'u'lláh returned to Baghdad after his two-year sojourn in the mountains of Kurdistan.

Again Bahá'u'lláh writes of this time and of his realization that his own destiny, with all of its inherent difficulties, was not subject to his own will but to the will of God:

> We knew not . . . that the mesh of divine destiny exceedeth the vastest of mortal conceptions, and the dart of His [God's] decree transcendeth the boldest of human designs. None can escape the snares He setteth, and no soul can find release except through submission to His will. By the righteousness of God! Our withdrawal contemplated no return, and Our separation hoped for no reunion. The one object of Our retirement was to avoid becoming a subject of discord among the faithful, a source of disturbance unto Our companions, the means of injury to any soul, or the cause of sorrow to any heart. Beyond these, We cherished no other intention, and apart from them, We had no end in view. And yet, each person schemed after his own desire, and pursued his own idle fancy, until the hour when, from the Mystic Source, there came the summons bidding Us return whence We came. Surrendering Our will to His, We submitted to His injunction.[7]

As soon as Bahá'u'lláh returned to Baghdad he began the arduous work of reunifying the splintered Bábí community. His presence strengthened and revitalized the believers, and as his reputation grew, all sorts of visitors began calling on him. People were now coming from Kurdistan, where he had become a legend. Bahá'u'lláh's humble residence, located in the old quarter of the city, became a center of attraction. Even those who were accustomed to palaces, including Persian royalty, came to him oblivious of the simplicity of his living conditions. Being with him was all that mattered. Even the city's leading clergy and its governor sought his counsel. The British diplomatic representative was so enamored of Bahá'u'lláh that he offered him British citizenship and permanent residence in India.

For the next seven years Bahá'u'lláh's presence strengthened and rebuilt the Bábí community in Baghdad while his messages helped to unify the Bábís in Persia. Many people traveled long distances, some on foot, to visit Bahá'u'lláh. They went back to their villages and cities spiritually rejuvenated, wanting to share their experiences with those who could not make the trip. This simple process had a solidifying effect on the Bábís. They now had someone to rally around.

Among those who called on Bahá'u'lláh was a representative of some of the leading Muslim scholars of Persia. They had heard of Bahá'u'lláh's reputation and wanted to test his wisdom. The representative was deeply impressed with Bahá'u'lláh's responses to the questions he put to him, but to test Bahá'u'lláh further the representative asked him to perform a miracle. Only then, he explained, would the scholars accept Bahá'u'lláh's authority. To this man's great surprise, Bahá'u'lláh consented to the request on the condition that the group must unanimously choose one miracle for him to perform. Furthermore, if he performed the miracle, they were to promise in writing that they would accept him and would acknowledge and confess the truth of his cause publicly. If the miracle was performed, no doubt would remain for them, and if not, Bahá'u'lláh would be convicted of imposture.

The representative carried this agreement back to the scholars. However, after many days of debate, the scholars were unable to agree on what miracle they wanted Bahá'u'lláh to perform. They had no choice but to drop their demand. News of this incident spread throughout Persia and Iraq, enhancing Bahá'u'lláh's reputation still further. But still he did not make his mission known. Only God could deem when that was to be announced.

Despite the high esteem most people held for Bahá'u'lláh, there were still those whose jealousy and love of power led them to want to harm him. One of these individuals was a priest who collaborated with the Persian consul-general of Baghdad in a plan to rid the city of Bahá'u'lláh.

The consul-general hired a local ruffian to murder Bahá'u'lláh. The cutthroat followed his prey, waiting for the right moment to carry out his assignment. That moment came one day while Bahá'u'lláh was in the public bath. As the assassin approached his target, however, he was overcome by Bahá'u'lláh's presence and fled the scene, trembling.

The assassin tried again, for the reward that had been promised was great. One day after he had recovered his nerve he spotted Bahá'u'lláh in the street with an attendant. But again the assassin was unable to carry out his assignment. Standing before Bahá'u'lláh, he was struck with such fear that he dropped his revolver and found himself unable to move, as if he were paralyzed. Bahá'u'lláh approached his would-be assailant and said to his attendant, "Pick up his pistol and give it to him, and show him the way to his house; he seems to have lost his way."[8]

During the years Bahá'u'lláh lived in Baghdad he wrote profusely. His was not an ordinary writing approach. When revelation came to him, without hesitation words flowed from his lips, requiring the help of a secretary to keep up with the speed at which they came forth, filling page after page. In one instance, over the course of two days and two nights, he revealed one of his most important works, a volume of some two hundred pages called the Book of Certitude (commonly referred to by its Arabic title, *The Kitáb-i-Íqán*).

The Book of Certitude contains the basic tenets of the Bahá'í Faith. It proclaims that there is one God, Who is the source of all divine revelation, and explains the role of the Divine Educators and their mission in the history of society. In this book Bahá'u'lláh asserts the essential unity of the Divine Educators, affirming the universality of their spiritual message, the identity of their fundamental teachings, the sacredness of their scriptures, and the twofold character of their stations. He explains the meaning of allegorical passages from the Bible and the Koran that have for centuries been misunderstood by religious leaders, sweeping away barriers that have separated the world's religions and laying the foundation for the reconciliation of their followers.

The book is an appeal for humanity to earnestly seek spiritual truth and break down the barriers that have kept people of differing faiths apart. Bahá'u'lláh writes,

> Only when the lamp of search, of earnest striving, of longing desire, of passionate devotion, of fervid love, of rapture, and ecstasy, is kindled within the seeker's heart, and the

> breeze of His [God's] loving-kindness is wafted upon his soul, will the darkness of error be dispelled, the mists of doubts and misgivings be dissipated, and the lights of knowledge and certitude envelop his being. At that hour will the mystic Herald . . . awaken the heart, the soul, and the spirit from the slumber of negligence. Then will the manifold favours and outpouring grace of the holy and everlasting Spirit confer such new life upon the seeker that he will find himself endowed with a new eye, a new ear, a new heart, and a new mind. He will contemplate the manifest signs of the universe, and will penetrate the hidden mysteries of the soul. Gazing with the eye of God, he will perceive within every atom a door that leadeth him to the stations of absolute certitude.[9]

Other books were also revealed during this period. Among them is *The Hidden Words,* a collection of short yet profound verses that holds a position of unsurpassed importance among Bahá'u'lláh's ethical writings. Bahá'u'lláh describes this work, saying, "This is that which hath descended from the realm of glory, uttered by the tongue of power and might, and revealed unto the Prophets of old. We have taken the inner essence thereof and clothed it in the garment of brevity, as a token of grace unto the righteous, that they may stand faithful unto the Covenant of God, may fulfill in their lives His trust, and in the realm of spirit obtain the gem of divine virtue." The verses touch upon themes such as why God created humanity, what it takes to secure His love, and the importance of humanity's response to divine counsel. They not only offer a source of profound spiritual inspiration and deep insight into the purpose of life but also a code to live by. The following lines from *The Hidden Words* serve as a characteristic example from the collection of verses in the book: "O Son of Spirit! My first counsel is this: Possess a pure, kindly and radiant heart, that thine may be a sovereignty ancient, imperishable and everlasting."[10]

Another important work of Bahá'u'lláh's from this period is a mystical composition titled The Seven Valleys. It describes the seven spiritual stages the human soul must traverse in its quest to draw nearer to God and fulfill the purpose of life. Bahá'u'lláh writes, "The stages that mark the wayfarer's journey from the abode of dust to the heavenly homeland are said to be seven. . . . And they say that until the wayfarer taketh leave of self, and traverseth these stages, he shall never reach to the ocean of nearness and union, nor drink of the peerless wine."[11]

7
THE PROMISED DAY

By 1863 Bahá'u'lláh's popularity had grown to such a degree that it led to his expulsion from Baghdad. The shah of Persia was persuaded by members of the government who saw Bahá'u'lláh as a threat to ask the Turkish sultan to remove Bahá'u'lláh from the city. These detractors claimed that Bahá'u'lláh's still relatively close proximity to Persia was endangering Persian security. Constantinople (now Istanbul), the capital of the mightiest empire in the Middle East, was to be the next stop in Bahá'u'lláh's odyssey.

News of Bahá'u'lláh's impending departure spread throughout Baghdad, giving rise to much sorrow in the city. Its most prominent clergyman, with tears in his eyes, called on Bahá'u'lláh to bid him farewell. The clergyman denounced the shah for instigating Bahá'u'lláh's removal from his city. The governor of Baghdad also called on Bahá'u'lláh. Grief-stricken, he deplored Bahá'u'lláh's leaving and asked what he could do for him. Bahá'u'lláh urged him to treat the Bábís of Baghdad with kindness.

Further difficulties were in store for Bahá'-u'lláh and his family. Constantinople would not be the last place to which he would be exiled, nor would it be an easy place to live. Further trials and turmoil lay ahead. A dream he had shortly before he left Baghdad seemed to confirm this:

> I saw the Prophets and the Messengers gather and seat themselves around Me, moaning, weeping and loudly lamenting. Amazed, I inquired of them the reason, whereupon their lamentation and weeping waxed greater, and they said unto Me: "We weep for Thee, O Most Great Mystery, O Tabernacle of Immortality!" They wept with such a weeping that I too wept with them. Thereupon the Concourse on high addressed Me saying: ". . . Erelong shalt Thou behold with Thine own eyes what no prophet hath beheld. . . . Be patient, be patient." . . . They continued addressing Me the whole night until the approach of dawn.[1]

Aware of Bahá'u'lláh's prominence in Baghdad, the Turkish prime minister wanted to avoid giving the impression that Bahá'u'lláh was being forced to leave the city, as that would arouse the populace. Instead, everyone was led to believe that the sultan himself had simply invited Bahá'u'lláh to live in Constantinople. In fact, the deputy-governor was instructed to give Bahá'u'lláh a relatively large sum of money along with the invitation to travel to Constantinople with an armed escort. Though Bahá'u'lláh accepted the invitation, he refused to take the money. When the deputy-governor urgently appealed to him not to refuse the funds lest the authorities be offended, he reluctantly accepted the money and then distributed it to the poor.

Twelve days before leaving Baghdad Bahá'u'lláh moved to a large garden just outside of the city. During the twelve days he spent in the garden, Bahá'u'lláh proclaimed his mission to his closest friends and companions, a mission he had not divulged for ten trying years. He announced that he was the Divine Educator foretold by religions of old, the one whom people of different faiths and cultures all around the world had been awaiting—the one to whom the Báb had referred as "Him Whom God shall make manifest."

Aside from Bahá'u'lláh no one at that verdant spot during those twelve days in late April 1863 could fully appreciate the magnitude of what had happened when Bahá'u'lláh made this announcement. Bahá'ís today celebrate this twelve-day period annually as the most important of festivals. Bahá'u'lláh refers to the significance of his declaration, saying that "all created things were immersed in the sea of purification" and that the very atoms of the earth were affected.[2] It was as if a great rush of energy had been unleashed from a source that no ordinary mortal could comprehend or reach. Some people today are beginning to appreciate what has happened in the world since Bahá'u'lláh made his divinely inspired announcement. Indeed, many believe that evidence of this great release of spiritual energy can be seen in the astonishing number of advances the world has enjoyed in all fields of human endeavor since 1863.

The mission of Bahá'u'lláh was dramatic and transformative on many levels. Not only did he speak of uniting the peoples of the world and overcoming the many social ills that plague human society, but he also spoke of transforming the hearts of individuals so that they might draw closer to God and thereby attain their true purpose for living. He called for more than an ideological acceptance of the oneness of humanity, summoning all people to a fundamentally spiritual change of heart, which he said was the next step in the evolution of humankind. Bahá'u'lláh writes,

> This is the Day in which God's most excellent favors have been poured out upon men, the Day in which His most mighty grace hath been infused into all created things. It is incumbent upon all the peoples of the world

> to reconcile their differences, and, with perfect unity and peace, abide beneath the shadow of the Tree of His care and loving-kindness. It behoveth them to cleave to whatsoever will, in this Day, be conducive to the exaltation of their stations, and to the promotion of their best interests. . . .
>
> Beseech ye the one true God to grant that all men may be graciously assisted to fulfill that which is acceptable in Our sight. Soon will the present-day order be rolled up, and a new one spread out in its stead. Verily, thy Lord speaketh the truth, and is the Knower of things unseen.[3]

During the last few days that Bahá'u'lláh remained in the garden near Baghdad, many people came to visit one last time and bid him farewell. In fact, his departure resembled a public farewell to an adored king, not that of an exiled prisoner. A multitude of well-wishers gathered at the garden—Bábís, Jews, Christians, and Muslims alike—many straining to catch a glimpse of him, some prostrating themselves before him. Ten Turkish soldiers headed the departing caravan, which included Bahá'u'lláh's family and a few followers. His scheming half-brother and a few of his cohorts followed behind.

It took nearly four months by land and sea to reach Constantinople, the capital of the

Ottoman Empire. Wherever the party stopped on their travels they were treated royally. At one place they were greeted by a legion of army drummers who escorted them into town, where the eager inhabitants awaited the wise one of whom they had heard so much.

Bahá'u'lláh's stay in Constantinople was to be very short-lived. The Persian diplomats in the Ottoman capital found his presence just as threatening as the Persian diplomats and clergymen in Baghdad had. His refusal to engage with the sultan's ministers in the customary exchange of visits and political favors made it easy for the Persian ambassador to engineer Bahá'u'lláh's further banishment to a more remote location. After only four months in Constantinople, Bahá'u'lláh, his family, and their small group of companions were ordered to move on to Adrianople (now known as Edirne) in December 1863. It took twelve grueling days to get there, traveling through snow and freezing temperatures. Although he had never been charged with any crime, Bahá'u'lláh was now officially a prisoner.

Despite the tightening restrictions, Bahá'u'lláh pressed on in Adrianople with his mission, which began to take a global turn. Having already declared his mission to his closest friends and companions, he now began to raise his voice to the world, proclaiming his identity and purpose through letters to the world's mightiest secular and religious leaders. It was during this period that the Bábís who accepted Bahá'u'lláh's announcement of his mission began to refer to themselves as Bahá'ís, or followers of Bahá'u'lláh.

Among the first of these major letters was a call to the kings and rulers of the world to embrace Bahá'u'lláh's message and recognize his word as the Voice of God. He exhorted the leaders, among other things, to be just and vigilant, to overcome their differences, to reduce their armaments, and to care for the poor. Failure to heed this appeal, he warned, would lead to divine chastisement:

> Beware not to deal unjustly with anyone that appealeth to you, and entereth beneath your shadow. Walk ye in the fear of God, and be ye of them that lead a godly life. Rest not on your power, your armies, and treasures. Put your whole trust and confidence in God, Who hath created you, and seek ye His help in all your affairs. . . .
>
> Know ye that the poor are the trust of God in your midst. Watch that ye betray not His trust, that ye deal not unjustly with them and that ye walk not in the ways of the treacherous. Ye will most certainly be called upon to answer for His trust on the day when the Balance of Justice shall be set, the day when unto everyone shall be rendered his

> due, when the doings of all men, be they rich or poor, shall be weighed.
>
> If ye pay no heed to the counsels which, in peerless and unequivocal language, We have revealed in this Tablet, Divine chastisement shall assail you from every direction, and the sentence of His justice shall be pronounced against you.[4]

Other messages of a similar character were addressed to the heads of state of Great Britain, France, Germany, Austria-Hungary, Russia, the American republics, the Ottoman Empire, and Persia. Each message was different, focusing on the particular needs and conditions of the recipient's country. They were powerful pronouncements given as a physician prescribes a course of treatment to an epidemic-stricken community. There was a ring of urgency to the messages. For example, to the sultan of the Ottoman Empire he wrote,

> Let My counsel be acceptable to thee, and strive thou to rule with equity among men, that God may exalt thy name and spread abroad the fame of thy justice in all of the world. Beware lest thou aggrandize thy ministers at the expense of thy subjects. Fear the sighs of the poor and of the upright in heart who, at every break of day, bewail their

plight, and be unto them a benignant sovereign. They, verily, are thy treasures on earth. It behoveth thee, therefore, to safeguard thy treasures from the assaults of them who wish to rob thee. Inquire into their affairs, and ascertain, every year, nay every month, their condition, and be not of them that are careless of their duty. . . .

It behoveth every king to be as bountiful as the sun, which fostereth the growth of all beings, and giveth to each its due, whose benefits are not inherent in itself, but are ordained by Him Who is the Most Powerful, the Almighty. The king should be as generous, as liberal in his mercy as the clouds, the outpourings of whose bounty are showered upon every land, by the behest of Him Who is the Supreme Ordainer, the All-Knowing.[5]

Unfortunately, few of the leaders who were addressed chose to heed Bahá'u'lláh's warnings and admonitions. Those who ignored or rejected his appeals found themselves unable to withstand the thrusts of this tumultuous period in history. At the worst, their rule would not endure; at the least their royal houses would experience upheaval.

With the world's leaders choosing not to take the path Bahá'u'lláh advised them to take, he predicted that a "lesser peace"—a global peace born out of political and economic necessity rather than from a spiritual acknowledgment of our oneness as a race—would eventually be forged, but not without much travail and sorrow. A much greater and enduring universal peace, Bahá'u'lláh explained, would materialize only when humanity is spiritually unified, when all people will view each other as children of God and will fully understand what that implies.

Only one sovereign did not denounce Bahá'u'lláh's message and his claim to be the Divine Educator for this day. After reading the message Bahá'u'lláh addressed to her, Queen Victoria is reported to have commented, "'If this is of God, it will endure; if not, it can do no harm.'"[6]

After almost five years in Adrianople Bahá'u'lláh's life as an exile and prisoner was to take yet another turn. In a state of paranoia, the sultan of the Ottoman Empire was persuaded to believe rumors and accusations he was receiving from Bahá'u'lláh's jealous half-brother and his supporters. They alleged that Bahá'u'lláh was conspiring with several ministers of European governments to overthrow the sultanate. These attacks caused Bahá'u'lláh no end of grief. Though the days he had spent in the Black Pit of Tehran had been physically torturous, nothing grieved him more than the machinations of his envious brother and his supporters in Adrianople. The suffering that Bahá'u'lláh had endured in Tehran had been at the hands of external enemies, while the suffering he endured in Adrianople was caused by those who claimed to love him.

In August 1868 the sultan took drastic action, issuing an edict calling for Bahá'u'lláh's banishment to the prison-city of Acre, Palestine (now Israel), where he was to serve out a life sentence. This was to be the last point on Bahá'u'lláh's long path of exile, for he would spend the remainder of his life in this city and its outlying area in the Holy Land. At the same time, Bahá'u'lláh's half-brother was banished to Cyprus, where he eventually died a broken, lonely man.

The journey to Acre by land and sea took nineteen days. Traveling in the heat of the summer, Bahá'u'lláh and his companions arrived in Acre exhausted. By 1868 Acre, an ancient city, was in serious decline. Once known as the Bastille of the Middle East, it was now little more than a penal colony to which the Ottoman Empire's most dangerous criminals and political enemies were sent. It was an inhospitable place. Parched and devoid of fresh water and greenery, the city was known for its foul air. Conditions were so bad that, according to legend, any bird flying over the city would drop dead.

When Bahá'u'lláh reached Acre he was greeted by hostile onlookers who mocked him, calling him "the God of the Persians." He and his family as well as the others who had accompanied them on their journey, some seventy people in all, were herded into two dirty cells without beds. Bahá'u'lláh recounts, "The first night, all were deprived of either food or drink . . . They even begged for water, and were refused."[7] The days that followed brought no improvements, only a daily ration of salty bread and brackish water. Malaria and dysentery plagued the prisoners. Within a few days of their arrival in Acre, three people died. It was clear that the sultan's intention was to still the voice of Bahá'u'lláh forever.

Nevertheless Bahá'u'lláh continued to write to world leaders, including Pope Pius IX. "Leave thou the world behind thee," was his appeal to the pope, "and turn towards thy Lord, through Whom the whole earth hath been illumined. . . . Dwellest thou in palaces whilst He Who is the King of Revelation liveth in the most desolate of abodes?" Bahá'u'lláh added, "This is the day whereon the Rock (Peter) crieth out and shouteth, and celebrateth the praise of its Lord, the All-Possessing, the Most High, saying: 'Lo! The Father is come, and that which ye were promised in the Kingdom is fulfilled! . . .' My body longeth for the cross, and Mine head waiteth the thrust of the spear, in the path of the All-Merciful, that the world may be purged from its transgressions. . . ."[8]

Not surprisingly, the pope chose to ignore Bahá'u'lláh's call. In fact, after Bahá'u'lláh revealed this message, the pope in 1870 issued the decree of papal infallibility, which states that the pope cannot err when speaking in the exercise of his office to define a doctrine of Christian faith or morals. Two months later the Italian army seized all of the Papal States and succeeded in stripping the Roman Catholic church of its temporal authority in Italy, relegating its center to a small area within Rome. A brooding and depressed Pope Pius IX became known as the Prisoner of the Vatican.

Other messages were addressed to the Christian, Muslim, Jewish, and Zoroastrian priesthoods. But not one elicited a positive response. In Iran, however, the Bahá'ís grew more united. As they intensified their efforts to share Bahá'u'lláh's message, their numbers swelled. Despite Bahá'u'lláh's imprisonment in a far-off land, the Bahá'ís rejoiced in the knowledge that "Him Whom God shall make manifest" had indeed appeared and that his guidance flowed to them in the messages that he wrote and sent to them. For some, these wonderful writings deepened their desire to meet Bahá'u'lláh. They felt they had to go to the Holy Land, perchance they could meet him.

These ardent believers traveled for months, often on foot, through the scorching deserts and freezing mountains of Iran, Iraq, and Syria. When they reached Acre, restrictions were sometimes so strict that they could not enter the prison-city and had to be satisfied with a glimpse of Bahá'u'lláh's hand waving to them from the barred window of his prison cell. Yet even then they would return to Iran feeling spiritually renewed and praying that the harsh restrictions would not last much longer.

After more than two years inside the prison, Bahá'u'lláh and his family were transferred to a house outside the prison's walls. However, they still were not free to leave the area.

In time, the shackles of the Ottomans began to crack. Acre's chief religious leader, once an avowed enemy of Bahá'u'lláh, embraced his cause. The governor of Acre begged Bahá'u'lláh for the opportunity to do something for him. Bahá'u'lláh responded by observing that if the aqueduct outside Acre were repaired, the quality of the city's drinking water would improve and would benefit the people's health. The governor carried out Bahá'u'lláh's wish.

Many of the inhabitants of Acre attributed the improved quality of air to Bahá'u'lláh's presence among them. From fanatical opposition, they had grown to revere the distinguished prisoner.

For nine years Bahá'u'lláh remained confined to the same house, writing profusely and receiving visitors as permitted. Among the writings he produced at this time is a work titled *The Kitáb-i-Aqdas,* meaning in Arabic "The Most Holy Book."

After these nine years of confinement it became possible for Bahá'u'lláh to leave the prison-city. Through the efforts of his eldest son and those of the governor of Acre and the city's leading clergyman, all of whom wanted to make Bahá'u'lláh's life happier, he was persuaded to move to a house outside the city's walls. The governor assured Bahá'u'lláh that he could go anywhere he pleased in the region. Bahá'u'lláh settled in a house on the outskirts of Acre, enjoying greater freedom than he had in years.

In the twilight of his life, though nominally still a prisoner of the Ottoman Empire, four times Bahá'u'lláh was able to set out from his home to visit the city of Haifa, situated on the side of Mount Carmel. In 1891 on one of these visits he pitched his tent on its slopes and remained there for three months.

Mount Carmel had been the focus of considerable attention earlier in the century. Many

German Adventist Christians had given up their homes and jobs to establish a colony at the foot of Mount Carmel, certain that Christ's return was imminent and that Mount Carmel was the place where he would appear. Other Christian Adventist groups shared that view. One of the Germans inscribed over his front door the words *Der Herr ist Nahe,* meaning "The Lord is Near." On top of Mount Carmel, near the Cave of Elijah, stood the Carmelite Monastery, its monks poised for the second coming of Christ.

Bahá'u'lláh passed the German colony several times during his visits to Haifa and even stayed in one of the houses in the colony. At one point he climbed the mountain and pitched his tent on its slopes. Entering the Cave of Elijah on this occasion, he proclaimed: "Call out to Zion, O Carmel, and announce the joyful tidings: He that was hidden from mortal eyes is come! His all-conquering sovereignty is manifest; His all-encompassing splendor is revealed."[9]

For many Jews the period when Bahá'u'lláh was living in the Holy Land was highly significant. In the mid- and late-1800s many Jews began to return to the Holy Land after the Edict of Toleration was signed by the British and Ottoman Empires in 1844, the very year in which the Báb had proclaimed his mission. This series of treaties annulled a twelve hundred-year-old pact between the Christians and Muslims which barred Jews from migrating to the Holy Land. Not long after the end of Bahá'u'lláh's imprisonment, the course of Jewish history was altered radically. The Jews' long yearning to return to Israel and fashion a homeland was realized. Bahá'u'lláh himself had prophesied the return of the Jews and the birth of modern Israel.

Among the many people who visited Bahá'u'lláh in the later years of his life was Cambridge University's professor E. G. Browne, the only Western scholar to interview Bahá'u'lláh. In his written account, Professor Browne shares the following:

> The face of him on whom I gazed I can never forget, though I cannot describe it. Those piercing eyes seemed to read one's very soul; power and authority sat on that ample brow; while the deep lines on the forehead and face implied an age which the jet-black hair and beard flowing down in indistinguishable luxuriance almost to the waist seemed to belie. No need to ask in whose presence I stood, as I bowed myself before One who is the object of a devotion and love which kings might envy and emperors sigh for in vain!
>
> A mild dignified voice bade me be seated, and then continued:—"Praise be to God that thou has attained! . . . Thou hast come to

see a prisoner and an exile . . . We desire but the good of the world and the happiness of the nations; yet they deem us a stirrer up of strife and sedition worthy of bondage and banishment . . . That all nations should become one in faith and all men as brothers; that the bonds of affection and unity between the sons of men should be strengthened; that diversity of religion should cease, and differences of race be annulled—what harm is there in this? . . . Yet so it shall be; these fruitless strifes, these ruinous wars shall pass away, and the 'Most Great Peace' shall come . . . Do not you in Europe need this also? Is not this that which Christ foretold? . . . Yet do we see your kings and rulers lavishing their treasures more freely on means for the destruction of the human race than on that which would conduce to the happiness of mankind . . . These strifes and this bloodshed and discord must cease, and all men be as one kindred and one family . . . Let not a man glory in this, that he loves his country; let him rather glory in this, that he loves his kind . . ."[10]

Bahá'u'lláh passed away peacefully on 29 May 1892, still officially a prisoner of the Ottoman Empire and a Persian exile. But many of the people in the area surrounding Acre did not regard him as such. To them, even those who did not accept his cause, he was their compassionate father. In some respects, Bahá'u'lláh had proven that he was mightier than one of the world's most powerful empires. Mysteriously, he had severed the yoke that had been placed on him and had steadfastly fulfilled his divine mission.

Christian, Jew, Muslim, priest, merchant, teacher, local men, women, children, poor, and rich—all flocked to Bahá'u'lláh's funeral, driven by a genuine love and admiration for one who had initially been mocked and scorned upon his arrival twenty-four years earlier.

Bahá'u'lláh's passing did not thwart the mission he had set out to achieve. The significance of this mission—which was nothing less than to bring about the complete spiritual transformation of the world and its inhabitants—would become apparent in time. He had done what God had willed him to do despite captivity and torture. And no earthly force, regardless of its might and power, has been able to stop what he set in motion: a movement that is spiritually transforming the world according to God's will.

8
OUR SPIRITUAL REALITY

If we were to look at the lives of the Báb and Bahá'u'lláh merely from a historical perspective, it would be easy to see their ministries as little more than a series of heroic feats and acts of sacrifice. However, to look at things this way would be to miss the point entirely.

Viewed from a spiritual perspective, the ministries of the Báb and Bahá'u'lláh can be seen as pure expressions of absolute faith in the Divine Will. Chosen by God to carry out their particular missions, the Báb and Bahá'u'lláh did so without hesitation and with complete devotion to God. Though their missions inevitably brought them a great deal of pain and suffering, they took solace in knowing that their contribution would help humanity to fulfill its destiny—its ultimate unification and the establishment of the kingdom of God on earth.

The Báb's mission was to herald and prepare the way for the coming of "Him Whom God shall make manifest": Bahá'u'lláh, whose mission, in turn, was to share God's will for humanity today by revealing the spiritual teachings that are needed to move humanity from its present stage of development to the next.

The stages of development in human society as a whole can be compared to the stages of individual human development, which include infancy, childhood, adolescence, and maturity. If we consider the history of humankind, many parallels can be seen. Humanity's present stage of development as a whole can be compared to the stage of adolescence, which is generally characterized by rapid change, conflicting desires, emotional turbulence, and growing maturity. The revelation of Bahá'u'lláh is intended to enable humanity to advance from adolescence to maturity by providing individuals with the spiritual light needed to lead them out of the darkness of uncertainty, suspicion, and fear to become enlightened children of God. When this happens, they draw inspiration from the Supreme Parent and become a force for unity in their communities.

Bahá'u'lláh's teachings describe the essence of human nature, define our purpose in life, and emphasize the oneness of humanity. They also provide guidance on how to discover and develop one's true self. Those who take to heart these aspects of Bahá'u'lláh's message enjoy a newfound sense of assurance and confidence. They look upon life as an exciting, enriching challenge, viewing every day as a new opportunity to draw closer to God and to serve their fellow human beings. Approaching life in this way becomes so uplifting, so exhilarating and confirming that we begin to want to do everything we can to adhere to Bahá'u'lláh's guidance, because we are certain that it comes from God.

The following appeal by Bahá'u'lláh describes the vision of what every human being is capable of becoming:

> Be generous in prosperity, and thankful in adversity. Be worthy of the trust of thy neighbor, and look upon him with a bright and friendly face. Be a treasure to the poor, an admonisher to the rich, an answerer of the cry of the needy, a preserver of the sanctity of thy pledge. Be fair in thy judgment, and guarded in thy speech. Be unjust to no man, and show all meekness to all men. Be as a lamp unto them that walk in darkness, a joy to the sorrowful, a sea for the thirsty, a haven for the distressed, an upholder and defender of the victim of oppression. Let integrity and uprightness distinguish all thine acts. Be a home for the stranger, a balm to the suffering, a tower of strength for the fugitive. Be eyes to the blind, and a guiding light unto the feet of the erring. Be an ornament to the countenance of truth, a crown to the brow of fidelity, a pillar of the temple of righteousness, a breath of life to the body

> of mankind, an ensign of the hosts of justice, a luminary above the horizon of virtue, a dew to the soil of the human heart, an ark on the ocean of knowledge, a sun in the heaven of bounty, a gem on the diadem of wisdom, a shining light in the firmament of thy generation, a fruit upon the tree of humility.[1]

While most of us would love to be all of the things that Bahá'u'lláh asks us to be, it is understandable that after first reading this appeal we may quickly conclude that it is impossible to attain such virtuousness. Most would say it is too much to ask of anyone. While that may seem to be a reasonable assessment, Bahá'u'lláh, as the Divine Educator for this day, would not have made the appeal if he did not believe that humans have the potential to become all of these things. He is aware of our true nature, while most of us have an incomplete or distorted view of what that really is.

In most cases our physical nature dominates our spiritual nature. This has been the cause of much of the misery and mayhem that humans have experienced over the ages. We desperately need to reverse this dominance so that our spiritual nature prevails over our physical nature. Bahá'u'lláh helps us understand this by explaining comprehensively the true essence and purpose of human life. Internalizing this knowledge transforms our lives spiritually and enables us to become what we were meant to be.

Most of us are not what we think we are. Many people believe that human beings are primarily animals with superior brains, that life is essentially a jungle, and that humans, because of their unequaled intelligence, are the leading predators. To support this argument they point to the wars, bloody revolutions, and atrocities that have plagued humanity and to the raping of the planet's forests, the annihilation of its animal and plant species, and the brazen pollution of its air and water. The rational among them seek ways to curb what they feel is humanity's natural tendency toward aggression and violence. To achieve their aim they try to create an atmosphere of tolerance. But in the end, that is not enough, for tolerance is a fragile condition. All it does is suspend aggression and violence. Because it does not address the underlying attitudes that are the root of the problem, people run out of tolerance and revert to their old, socially destructive ways.

Most people believe they have a soul, but they may not fully understand its reality—that is, they do not know its function, its precious properties, or its relationship with the body. Some adhere to the belief of certain medieval theologians that the soul can be found literally in the human heart. Because most people have a vague and somewhat distorted concept of the soul, it has come to be associated with certain material things such as food and music. One American car manufacturer has even advertised one of its models as having a soul.

There are others who are so confused over the clashing views about human nature that they simply never think about it, taking their spiritual reality for granted much as a fish takes for granted the water it swims in. These people lack the desire to experience spiritual fulfillment because it is a notion that is foreign to them.

Bahá'u'lláh has commented on this condition in his writings. Though he came to deliver God's message, he found humanity locked in a "strange stupor," "wandering in the paths of delusion, bereft of discernment to see God with their own eyes, or hear His Melody with their own ears." He found that their superstitions had become "veils between them and their own hearts and kept them from the path of God."[2] He found humanity treading paths leading them away from God and His desire for humanity.

Many people today seem unaware that the path to God exists within each human being. Much frenetic energy has been expended in recent years to find the right path, resulting in the development of thousands of schemes that have led people farther away from what they are seeking. Bahá'u'lláh points out that God is "closer to man than his life-vein." He even appeals to us to look within, saying, "Turn thy sight unto thyself, that thou mayest find Me standing within thee, mighty, powerful and self-subsisting."[3]

Could there be any greater tragedy than the fact that so many of the six billion human beings living and working on our planet do not fully understand their spiritual identity and do not know their purpose in life? Bereft of an awareness of the inherent nobility and wealth of potentialities in every one of us, we search aimlessly for hope. Without knowledge of the divine gifts within us, we are unable to draw upon the limitless reservoir of love that God has bestowed on each of us. Instead we rely on survival instincts such as fear, self-centeredness, and the need for supremacy over others, and we employ tolerance to protect our own interests.

If the great majority of women and men were to truly understand their purpose in life there would be no racism, sexism, ethnic cleansing campaigns, anti-Semitism, environmental pollution, abject poverty, capital greed, gangland feuds, white-collar crime, or genocidal wars. The personal and collective peace that all of the great Prophets of the past foretold would be realized. The point is that human beings have the means within them to create a saner, healthier world in which all can achieve happiness. Doesn't the Lord's Prayer indicate that one day we will realize the planetary condition implied in the phrase "Thy kingdom come"?

> Our Father, which art in heaven, Hallowed be thy name. Thy kingdom come. Thy will be done in earth as *it is* in heaven. Give us this day our daily bread. And forgive us our debts, as we forgive our debtors. And lead us not into temptation, but deliver us from evil: For thine is the kingdom, and the power, and the glory, for ever.[4]

Unfortunately, many people of good will have been seized by a sense of hopelessness and no longer believe this divine promise will be fulfilled. One of the reasons for Bahá'u'lláh's coming is to assure humankind that the Lord's Prayer will be fulfilled. This is why Bahá'u'lláh has placed such heavy emphasis on the importance of understanding our spiritual reality and fulfilling our true potential. Many who are heeding his words are finding encouragement and hope, for he has revealed a spiritual path that is bringing them closer to God and thus closer to fulfilling their purpose in life.

Several years ago while on a lecture tour in the United Kingdom, I witnessed the reaction of a group of people who, possibly for the first time, were hearing about the true nature of a human being. I saw the sparkle of hope unfold on their faces, which I sensed had reflected hopelessness throughout their lives.

I met these people at a job skills development center in an industrial suburb of Liverpool. I had been asked to give an inspirational talk emphasizing a religious theme. When I met the audience I was going to address, I realized that they were not in the mood for religion. They were unemployed, on welfare, angry, and had no hope of extricating themselves from their present condition. Their demeanor and speech revealed that they felt trapped, resigned to continue the same routines of life that their parents and their grandparents before them had carried out: holding a job in one of the town's factories, having as many children as they could bear, following a favorite soccer team, playing darts at the local pub. It seemed that they had no spiritual inclination, no conscious interest in even considering the question of what a human being is. They seemed to be victims of a distorted view of reality that had been passed down to them, acting as consenting captives in a prison called life.

It seemed as if most of them had given up on the religion of their forefathers and were leaning toward Marxism, a philosophy that was being openly espoused by the center's young, restless, and frustrated university-trained instructors. Had I appeared with a long beard, dressed in a robe and wielding a sword like the Bolsheviks of decades past, asking them to join me in breaking into the prime minister's London residence to overthrow the government, they might very well have followed me enthusiastically.

What was I to talk to them about? The talk that I had been asked to give seemed inappropriate. In a flash, the thought of speaking to them about what a human being is came to mind. Without mentioning Bahá'u'lláh by name, I drew upon his explanations of what constitutes a human being. It felt right to me. Based on the audience's reaction, it proved to be right.

At first I had doubts about whether I had made the right decision. Many people in the audience seemed skeptical, some even hostile; however, about halfway through the talk, many of them appeared to be genuinely interested. They became so interested that my thirty-minute scheduled stay was stretched to three hours. Even the cynical instructors showed genuine interest, skipping their usual four-o'clock break for tea.

They were so fascinated with the information I shared with them that they urged me to return the following day, but I couldn't because

I had to travel to another town. This was terribly frustrating to me, for I sensed that these people were experiencing a sense of hope that had thus far eluded them throughout their lives. Somehow I felt that they had gained a sense of what life could be like if they were to have the opportunity to study and internalize what I had shared with them.

The Bahá'í teachings point out that our true reality is spiritual—that we are a soul that happens to have a body and not merely a body that happens to have a soul. The distinction is subtle but great. While the body is subject to the laws of composition and decomposition—here today and gone tomorrow—the soul is everlasting. In other words, we are first and foremost, above all else, souls. That is our reality.

However, we often live as if our body were our true reality, giving far more attention to its care than to the development of our soul. This is understandable because we know so little about the soul. This does not mean we should abandon caring for our body, nor does it mean that the body and its many experiences are unimportant. Balance is required. When we understand the relationship of the soul and body, we develop a rational appreciation for the need to stay physically healthy.

The essence of the soul is a mystery, much like electricity is. You are not going to find electricity by cutting open an electric wire and examining it; similarly, you are not going to find the soul by cutting open the human body and looking inside. However, you will notice the attributes of electricity when you turn on a lamp. Similarly, the human body is a vehicle for the soul to manifest itself in this physical plane of existence. This is true even for those who do not believe in the existence of the soul, for a soulless body is a corpse.

Bahá'u'lláh teaches that the soul comes into being at the moment of conception. While the soul has a definite beginning, it has no end. Unlike the body, it is an intangible, single spiritual entity. It is immeasurable and indestructible. The soul is not inside the body; nor is it attached to it. In a sense, the soul's association with the body is much like that of a light focused on a mirror. You cannot pull the light out of the mirror. And even if the mirror should fall and break, the light will continue to shine.

Bahá'u'lláh also teaches that the soul is a spiritual emanation of God. This means there is a connection between each human soul and the life-creating, life-sustaining, unknowable essence called God—a connection that can be likened to the relationship between the sun and its rays. When humans ignore, reject, or remain unaware of the soul, they affect their connection with God, Who is a constant source of love and knowledge.

8—OUR SPIRITUAL REALITY

When we choose not to acknowledge our spiritual reality, we distance ourselves from God and from the good that constantly flows from the Almighty; distance from that source deprives and cripples the soul. The following verse from Bahá'u'lláh's writings expresses this truth: "O Son of Being! Love Me, that I may love thee. If thou lovest Me not, My love can in no wise reach thee. Know this, O servant."[5]

When a large number of people live this way—distancing themselves from God and His divine guidance—it can lead to serious troubles among individuals and communities. However, if enough people turn toward God and open themselves up to the constant flow of divine guidance, they will live in a community of loving harmony and will view service to one another as a privilege and a pleasure.

Inherent in the soul are certain qualities that most of us admire and wish we could demonstrate all the time. Truthfulness, compassion, love, integrity, selflessness, humility, fair-mindedness, and courtesy are some of these qualities. All of these and more are latent in the soul, just as the color, the fragrance, and the vitality of a flower are latent within the seed from which it develops. Every infant who comes into this world possesses these latent virtues.

Spiritual growth is organic, and the process of growth is unique for each individual. Sometimes the change within us is slow and subtle while at other times it is dramatic and swift. The divine virtues latent within the soul are like seeds that must be cultivated if they are to grow and reach their full potential. This requires proper and regular nourishment from the steady stream of God's knowledge and love. The source of this divine knowledge and love is God's chosen Spiritual Guide, or Divine Educator. In this day, that is Bahá'u'lláh. Turning to him and making sincere efforts to live according to his guidance for humanity nourishes our souls. As the Bahá'í writings state, "When a person becomes a Bahá'í, actually what takes place is that the seed of the spirit starts to grow in the human soul. This seed must be watered by the outpourings of the Holy Spirit. These gifts of the spirit are received through prayer, meditation, study of the Holy Utterances and service to the Cause of God."[6]

When the virtues latent in our souls are nourished regularly through prayer and daily efforts to live according to God's will, they become more prominent in our lives, eventually growing strong and permanent like the sturdy branches of a tree; we become virtuous women and men. We function as human beings are meant to function and become less prone to the negative behaviors and attitudes that lead to conflict, abuse, prejudice, lying, cheating, war, and other ills.

Bahá'u'lláh, like a divine physician, provides a prescription that specifies in detail how to nourish the virtues latent within us. When the prescription is applied regularly, we become more loving, compassionate, honest, truthful, selfless, service-minded, caring, thoughtful, and fair-minded.

The soul also possesses the powers of thought, comprehension, and imagination. Contrary to what most people may think, the human brain is not the same thing as the mind; the mind is an aspect of the soul. The brain is another organ in the human body, functioning as a central control mechanism to receive, store, and transmit messages from the mind. A damaged brain is unable to reflect the full scope of the mind, much like a faulty lamp transmits a flickering light.

One of the spiritual gifts that is unique to human beings is the ability to develop a penetrative sight that enables us to sense and perceive the reality of others. The powers of thought, comprehension, and imagination enable us to see beyond the laughing face that conceals a crying heart.

I once discovered this ability to sense the reality of others during an experience I had with one of my students. Josh, a twenty-seven year old who had just been released from the penitentiary, had matriculated into my academic program. The six-foot, seven-inch tall, 250-pound young man wanted desperately to succeed in life, especially for the sake of his six-year-old son, who had been abandoned by his heroin-dependent mother and cared for by the child's grandmother while Josh was in prison. The boy was now living with his father, a single parent who wanted to create a wholesome environment for his son and to be a healthy role model for him.

Josh was doing so well academically and showing such good leadership ability that I decided to break one of my cardinal rules, which was never to give a first-year student an internship. When I broke the good news to Josh, I was taken aback by his reaction.

"I'm not going!" he shouted, becoming mean and tight-lipped.

At first I was angry because I had gone out of my way to get Josh a choice internship, one that would draw him closer to realizing his career goal. But when I looked into Josh's angry eyes, I saw more fear than anger. I realized what Josh had really been saying even though his reaction was cloaked in anger: For the first time in his life he felt comfortable in school. For the first time in his life he was making good grades. If he were to take the internship and if someone were to treat him disrespectfully, he might lose his temper and end up hitting the person. This would mean going back to prison, and what would happen to his son?

I asked Josh to come to my office. Inside, the student sat ramrod straight, facing me, seething visibly with his tightly clenched fists planted on his lap. Though I felt uneasy—after all, the giant of a man before me had been in jail for assault and battery—I felt I had to find a way to penetrate Josh's armor. Fearful of saying the wrong thing, I resorted to prayer. It was the only thing I could do. I made a silent pact with God: "God, whatever passes from my lips, let it be guided by you and not from me." I looked into Josh's eyes and said suddenly, "If you don't take the internship, I'm going to kick your ass."

I was startled not only by what I had uttered, but by Josh's reaction. The young man began to cry, sobbing uncontrollably. I began to cry as well, because I realized that what Josh had heard wasn't so much what had passed from my lips but what had streamed from my heart. What Josh heard was, "I love you." And Josh had not heard that for a very long time. To him, I had become the father he never had. And he obeyed his father and took the internship.

I am no one special. All human beings have the capacity to do what I did. But if you are not aware of the capacity to reach out to others and sense their reality, it will go undeveloped, and you will continue to take things at face value. So much of reality, especially where human feelings are concerned, is carefully concealed.

Developing the ability to sense the reality of others hinges on one's progress in developing the latent virtues of the soul. When steady progress is made, the soul becomes more dominant and the body more submissive. In other words, the soul and body are united in understanding their primary purpose. Good, caring, and loving thoughts spring from the soul and are carried out by the body. For example, the idea of helping an elderly person to cross the street springs from the soul, and the body puts the idea into action. Or when we feel love for our children that feeling may emanate from our soul, but we express it with a hug or a word of encouragement.

When we begin to truly understand our spiritual reality, we become happier people. We feel more at peace with the world and what it has to offer to us. This understanding of our spiritual nature and how it draws us closer to God is not an ascetic sensibility, it is a joyful and tangible realization of our true destiny as children of God. It allows us to unite with others in ways that we could not have imagined, giving us a greater measure of happiness. It enables us to embrace that part of ourselves which is noblest. It is our faith made whole and our deepest hopes realized. It gives meaning and purpose to our lives.

9
THE PURPOSE OF LIFE

True freedom for an individual means becoming what you are meant to be. This has nothing to do with your career or where you live. You could be a ditch-digger or a prisoner and be free, or you could be a millionaire and not be free. One who truly understands what a human being is and earnestly strives to fulfill the purpose of life is experiencing true freedom. Of course, achieving our purpose in life—that is, achieving true freedom—hinges on truly understanding who and what we are as human beings. In chapter 8 we considered our spiritual reality and what it means to be truly human. Now we will consider what we must do to fulfill our purpose in life.

Most of us have never given much serious thought to our purpose in life. We have taken it for granted because we are preoccupied with the business of daily living, adapting to our environment and making the most of opportunities to live as comfortably as possible. Though most of us are surviving comfortably enough, we may have allowed ourselves to become so focused on material matters that we have forgotten there is something more to attend to. We have become so busy seeking to improve our style of life that we have ignored our spiritual needs.

But few of us really live in style, and even if we do, most of us, even the wealthy, sense that something is missing from our lives. That something can be found when we understand our purpose in life. No trips to far-flung locales noted for their spirituality are necessary to find what we are searching for. Though what we seek is spiritual, many of us have not found it in churches. We find our purpose when we engage in an important process that helps us reach our fullest potential as human beings. It is a process that has to become a part of our everyday lives, wherever we may be.

Fortunately, the process is simple, and there is guidance to help us. According to Bahá'í beliefs, there are three components to a person's purpose in life: strengthening our connection with God and drawing closer to Him, nurturing the latent divine qualities within us, and engaging in service to others to help improve the world.

It is important to develop an awareness of our connection to God because it is our lifeline, our "spiritual umbilical cord." The potency of that connection is dependent on the degree to which we know and love our Creator. The more we know and love God, the stronger our connection to Him becomes. There is a short but powerful prayer by Bahá'u'lláh that expresses this concept very clearly:

> I bear witness, O my God, that Thou hast created me to know Thee and to worship Thee. I testify, at this moment, to my powerlessness and to Thy might, to my poverty and to Thy wealth.
>
> There is none other God but Thee, the Help in Peril, the Self-Subsisting.[1]

As this connection to God grows stronger, we grow spiritually, and this aids the development of the divine qualities latent within our soul. When this happens, it becomes natural for us to actively help to make the world a better place in which to live. This does not mean that we have to become international philanthropists. We can make the world a better place by helping to improve the quality of life in our home, in our family, in our neighborhood, and at work and play.

It is important to note that all three components of our purpose in life are intertwined. For example, trying to make the world a better place without strengthening one's connection to God or without developing the virtues within us will ultimately end in failure. Sincere service to others arises from a genuine love for humanity and from a desire to exhibit the qualities that God wishes us to nurture—qualities such as trustworthiness, creativity, compassion, empathy, kindness, truthfulness, generosity, resourcefulness. These qualities of the soul must be developing steadily before they can be manifested to some degree. Furthermore, you cannot develop God-given virtues without drawing guidance from Him; that would be like trying to grow a garden without cultivating or nourishing it. When we make conscious efforts to draw closer to our Creator, the desire to develop virtues and be of service to our community inevitably follows.

If we depend solely on human will to achieve our purpose in life, we discover our limitations are greater and eventually find ourselves experiencing burnout and a loss of motivation. In contrast, drawing our energy from the Almighty continually fortifies our ability to develop divine virtues and serve our community constructively. Though the body of a highly spiritual person may grow tired, the soul remains inspired to develop its powers and qualities and to fulfill its destiny. When the soul has grown patient and compassionate, it can appreciate the need for the body to rest. But the reason for the rest and relaxation is to become more effective in developing virtues and helping to make the world a better place. When we are growing spiritually, we can experience joy regardless of the physical circumstances of our lives.

What keeps us from becoming engaged in the spiritual development process? Sometimes it is the condition of the community in which we live. When the majority of individuals in a community are preoccupied with material matters and give little or no thought to spiritual matters, their interactions create a collective consciousness that distances the members of the community from their true purpose in life. This is a condition that plagues most nations today.

Our communities do not have to be that way, however. Imagine creating a collective consciousness that is continually enriched by loving feelings, thoughts, opinions, and actions. It is possible, but it cannot be realized unless the majority of people gain an understanding of their true selves and of their purpose in life. Without such an understanding, the problems that plague the world today will only worsen.

But there is hope. The solution becomes a simple thing such as discovering one's true self—one's soul—and engaging in consistent efforts to develop it. This will produce a more balanced human being who will naturally become a force for good and unity in the community in which he or she lives. When enough individuals begin to do this, communities are transformed from centers of despair into bastions of enlightenment.

The story of Mehdi offers an example of how this can happen. Mehdi was a powerful human being. But not in the sense of a master body-builder. He was a spiritual powerhouse, because he was committed to mastering the three components to the purpose of life. Persecuted in his homeland of Iran because he was a Bahá'í, he was forced to leave and headed to America, leaving behind everything he owned except the clothing on his back and a satchel full of books, which he considered his lifeline to sanity.

He partook of the freedoms and opportunities that his adopted land afforded him. While grateful to America for the opportunity to pursue his profession as a scientist and live in relative safety, he was not blind to certain negative aspects of the American way of life. What disturbed him most was the racism. It was not directed against him, although during the Gulf War he was once denounced as a "dirty Iraqi" by a shopper in his neighborhood supermarket.

Because his laboratory was located in a poor African American section of the city, he became aware of the sense of helplessness and hopelessness that gripped most of the people who lived there. In many ways it reminded him of the south side of Tehran, whose inhabitants believed it was their destiny to live in squalor and despair. As a young university student at the University of Tehran, he had felt he should do something to help those people, and he did. Mehdi was able to persuade some college officials to allow him to teach at an elementary school where conditions were so bad that rats roamed freely in the unheated classrooms and often snatched the children's lunch bags.

Mehdi spent more than two years at that school, but he was ordered to leave it and never set foot on the premises again by an irate and fanatical local Islamic cleric who believed the Bahá'ís were agents of Satan.

In the United States, Mehdi's desire to serve the oppressed and those whose opportunities were limited by discrimination was as vigorous as when he lived in Iran—perhaps even greater. He jumped at every opportunity to serve, especially if it meant helping those who were victims of social injustice. He was not driven by a sense of pity or by a need for religious distinction. He did it to help humanity. Mehdi believed that all human beings were members of his family. Serving others was a way of expressing his love for God.

Troubled by the racism he observed in every area of his adopted land, he felt compelled to do something to help eliminate it. To do nothing, he believed, was unconscionable. Unfamiliar with the gravity of the problem and unaware of how it had started and developed over the years, he vowed to educate himself. He read books and audited two university-level African American history classes. When he began to frequent some of the African American restaurants in the neighborhood at night, some of his white professional colleagues urged him to stop the habit—they feared for his life.

Grateful for their concern, he nevertheless continued to pursue a campaign to become acquainted with the problem of racism. To appreciate it, he felt he needed to know African Americans and know them well enough to be trusted by them. Trust was necessary, he felt, in order to gain an appreciation of the depths of the wounds suffered by African Americans.

He made friends with a few individuals, and one in particular stood out: Milton. Without Milton's help, Mehdi would not have been able to carry out his personal battle against racism. As a young minister, fresh from the seminary, and full of idealism and enthusiasm, Milton pledged to support Mehdi's effort to recruit African American graduate students to work in his program and research project at his lab. In effect, Milton volunteered to be Mehdi's recruiter.

Mehdi's plan called for providing an opportunity for African Americans to earn PhDs in molecular genetic research. No African American student had ever earned such a degree at his university. Furthermore, the faculty and administration doubted that it was possible. Though they never voiced it openly, most of them felt that African Americans were incapable of functioning effectively in the physical sciences. When the dean heard of Mehdi's idea, he tried to discourage him from implementing it, claiming that it could retard his research and eventually cut off his rather substantial source of government funding.

Fortunately, Mehdi's contract with the government stated that he had sole jurisdiction as to who would be accepted into his graduate program and who would assist his research. Besides having their tuition paid for, the students who were accepted into the program would receive a $15,000 annual stipend.

Because of the cutting-edge research he was doing and the attractive financial package he was offering, Mehdi received about 250 applications for six openings. Most came from highly acclaimed graduates of the top American universities, and there were even a few from Oxford and Cambridge. Though none of the applicants was African American, Milton recruited two students who were. Roger was a graduate from an African American college in the South; Hakim, a young man from the neighborhood where the medical school was located, was a recent graduate from a state-supported city college that was noted more for its basketball team than for its quality of scholarship.

When the dean discovered that Mehdi had accepted the two African American applicants, who were statistically less qualified than the other applicants—in fact, one of them had done poorly on the Graduate Record Examination (GRE)—he became irate, unable to conceal his displeasure. In a matter of days, the school was rife with rumor, and Mehdi became the brunt of fellow faculty jokes. The most popular one was that Mehdi was now heading the "remedial research department."

While being the target of persistent backbiting was painful, Mehdi's commitment to carry out his campaign against racism never wavered. What hurt most was that Roger and Hakim were aware of the rumors and backbiting. Both Medhi and Milton spent hours with the two young men, shoring them up, assuring them that they could make it.

Hakim had the most doubts. Though he had taken the proper courses in college, he had not been exposed to the kind of academic rigor that was required of a physical science research program like Mehdi's. Mehdi believed that Hakim could succeed in his program because the young man had a genuine interest in genetics and possessed the kind of intuition that is needed for scientific breakthrough. As a consequence, Mehdi personally helped Hakim build up his physical science basics. At times he invited the young man to his suburban home, where the two would work all weekend on some of the things that Hakim should have learned in college.

Mehdi's intuition about Hakim proved correct. After a first-year struggle to keep pace with his Ivy League peers, Hakim, over the next three years, evolved into an academic star. Everything Mehdi sensed in the young man was realized.

During his third year, while assisting his professor, Hakim was struck with an idea that would require a separate course of investigation. When Mehdi learned about it, he encourage Hakim to pursue it, providing him with the facilities and funding to carry out his experiments.

It was not long before Hakim startled everyone in the department with a scientific breakthrough that became the subject of his doctoral dissertation. When news of Hakim's success reached the dean, the university's news bureau dispatched a reporter and photographer to Mehdi's laboratory to interview with the professor and his star pupil. A few days later the local news media asked for interviews. A picture of the dean with Mehdi and Hakim was circulated to the public through the university's news bureau.

With Hakim earning celebrity status, the backbiting directed at Mehdi ceased. No one, including the dean, questioned the professor's unorthodox admissions policy, which called for the admittance of two or three black students into his program every year.

To ensure that Mehdi's program would receive a continuing flow of graduate students, Milton launched a campaign to find high school seniors who demonstrated a sincere interest in biomedical sciences, followed them closely through their college years, and then guided them into Mehdi's program.

Milton made sure that what Mehdi had done did not escape the notice of the local African American community. He organized a banquet in Mehdi's and Hakim's honor, at which Hakim was the featured speaker. During his address Hakim turned to Mehdi, who was at the same table, and said, "I have never had a teacher who cares for me the way Mehdi does. He made it possible for me to learn to believe in myself. Without that I wouldn't have made it."

During Hakim's remarks, Mehdi silently thanked God for allowing him to serve his student. People like Mehdi—and there are few of them around—will not take credit for their achievements, because they view themselves as servants of God's will. Their greatest pleasure is derived from functioning in that capacity. Mehdi's attitude does not reflect a sense of self-loathing. On the contrary, he loves himself. But that love is not based on a belief that he is superior to others; it is based on an understanding of an important aspect of reality—his connection to God. He knows that if he dislikes himself, he dislikes God. Mehdi loves God. He knows that as a soul, he is a spiritual emanation of God. As he grows spiritually, his tie to his Creator strengthens, and he gains greater and greater access to the limitless reservoir of knowledge and love that is God. He taps into it as a means of solving problems and meeting life's challenges.

As we draw ever closer to God, developing the divine virtues that He has planted within us and in turn bestowing our gifts and service upon others, we find our purpose in life. The choice of what we will do, when we will do it, and how we will do it is ours alone to make. Only we can fulfill our God-given purpose in life.

10
THE SOUL'S JOURNEY

In chapters 8 and 9 we discussed what it means to be a human being and the purpose of life. Now we will consider the spiritual implications of living on this physical plane of existence.

Bahá'u'lláh points out that physical phenomena such as heat, cold, and suffering do not affect the soul—they only affect the body. Physical pain and anguish do not affect the essence of the soul. However, behaviors such as lying and backbiting do have an effect. Although they do not alter the nature of the soul, they will impede its ability to grow and manifest its inherent divine qualities, much like dust and smudges prevent a mirror from reflecting the full brilliance of a light that is shone on it. Removal of anything that impedes the soul's growth is dependent on our efforts to develop the soul's latent qualities. By gradually perfecting the virtues within us—becoming, for example, more consistently truthful, loving, courteous, humble, kind, generous—the soul eventually begins to dominate the body and its physical wants and needs, and we come closer to fulfilling our true potential as a human being.

Just as it is essential to clean a mirror regularly to prevent dust from collecting on its surface, it is essential to continue developing the soul's qualities and powers if we wish to grow spiritually. The development of the soul is a lifelong process.

The spiritual journey that we call "life" begins at the moment of conception. In the mother's womb the embryo develops body parts that will help it to survive and thrive in this world. Obviously, the human being was not meant to remain in its mother's womb indefinitely. Such body parts as arms, legs, eyes, and ears are developed in the womb, but they are intended to achieve their fullest potential beyond such confines. The fetus does not exercise free will; it is wholly dependent on its mother, who nourishes it through the umbilical cord.

However, once born, the child begins exercising its free will, albeit minimally. This becomes more pronounced at around two years of age and continues to develop as the child grows and matures. During adolescence children often flaunt their free will as a signal to their parents that they are about to cross the threshold leading into adulthood.

As a human being matures, he or she has the free will to choose to ignore the soul and rely solely on physical instincts to deal with life's myriad problems and challenges. Choosing that path, however, not only runs contrary to the course that God has destined for us but can also lead to disastrous results. To stay on course requires consistent efforts to develop the soul.

Just as a baby in the womb develops body parts that are to be used in this world, the human being is supposed to be developing his or her soul in this world for use in the life hereafter.

While the gestational period of a human baby is about nine months, the average natural life span for a human being in this world, barring accidental death or serious illness, is about eighty years. The divine virtues that a human being develops in this life are to be tried and tested before they are employed in the next life. The trying and testing is not merely an exercise regimen, for it has another purpose: to unite the human family and establish world peace. That ideal condition can be achieved if the great majority of human beings will exert themselves to develop the divine qualities latent within their souls.

In this physical part of the soul's journey—the here and now—life is a struggle. For those who repudiate or ignore their true essence and neglect their spiritual development, the struggle takes the form of materialistic competition or a sense of spiritual powerlessness. Success for such people is measured by the number of competitors they vanquish; the more victories they amass, the more successful they think they are. When the majority of a population engages in such a competitive struggle, a dog-eat-dog spirit prevails, creating the kind of society that we are all familiar with and want to free ourselves from. While struggle is a natural characteristic of life's journey in this plane of existence, it is not meant to be carried out on a battlefield or in the marketplace. The late social and religious thinker Horace Holley, author of *Religion for Mankind,* wrote, "the energy of personal struggle has been misunderstood and misapplied. The real purpose of that endowment is to equip the individual human being with capacity, not to overcome his fellow, but to transcend himself."[1]

Ideally, the human struggle is to be directed at overcoming the pull of our physical nature and achieving a more transcendent balance between our spiritual and physical natures. Continually nourishing the soul enables it to take its rightful place in its association with the body. This is not an easy task in the unsympathetic climate of a community obsessed with material pursuits. We are constantly challenged by the materialistic temptations, the countless tests, the personal physical drives that are stimulated by myriad images in modern media reflecting the profound absence of an active and dominant spiritual dimension in our lives.

As our spiritual awareness grows, we realize that spiritual development is a never-ending process. Life can be seen as an ongoing workshop in which continual strengthening of character takes place. The struggle does not end until we draw our very last breath.

The next phase of life's journey begins at death when we leave the womb of this world. At that point the association between body and soul ends, and the body returns to earth. Its substance is dispersed into the soil and atmosphere, and it becomes a part of other living things on the planet.

Unlike the body, the soul—that truest, most essential part of ourselves—enters into the next phase of its destiny, into the spiritual worlds of God. This is not a tangible place with pearly gates and angels floating about in white gowns, strumming golden harps. Nor is there a fiery place called hell, for heaven and hell are conditions, psychological and spiritual states of being—not literal places—that result from our spiritual progress or lack thereof.

Actually, we human beings in this physical plane of existence are like the fetus in the mother's womb, for we have no idea what the life hereafter is really like. But some clues have been given to us by the Spiritual Guides. A search of Bahá'í scripture reveals that once we pass into the life hereafter we find ourselves freed from all infirmities of body or mind and that we still possess whatever reasoning powers, knowledge, scientific achievements, wisdom, and insight we have attained while on this earthly plane. We become aware of many realities that were previously hidden from us and become able to comprehend all things with the eye of the soul, our inner eye.

Those souls who neglect their spiritual development in this physical world are able to progress in the life hereafter through the bounty of God, through the sincere prayers of others, and through acts of service performed in their name.

It is important to note that although I have described the spiritual journey of life by referring to the mother's womb, the here and now, and the life hereafter as if they were separate, distinct worlds, this is not the case. They are, in fact, only stages of development in the soul's journey through life. Because most of us rely on our physical senses to gain an understanding of reality, the world of the here and now appears separate from the purely spiritual world. In actuality, they are one and the same. All of creation is a single entity, but this does not become apparent until we pass into the next plane of existence.

10 — THE SOUL'S JOURNEY

Believing that the here and now is a world that is distinct and separate from the life hereafter is like believing that the world of the mother's womb is separate from the here and now. Though the child developing in the mother's womb cannot conceive of the world that lies outside, the child is nonetheless a part of this larger physical world. Only after birth does this aspect of reality become apparent to the child.

As we grow and mature, eventually we realize that while we were in our mother's womb, all that prevented us from experiencing the world outside was a relatively thin membrane. The same is true when we consider the idea that the life hereafter is not some entity that is distinctly separated from this plane of existence. Our heavy reliance on our physical senses creates veils that make it difficult for us to see and accept this aspect of reality.

The spiritually developing human being sometimes senses a natural connection with the next world. This has nothing to do with wanting to commit suicide. It is, rather, a yearning to improve one's spiritual condition in this world. The person who feels this way senses that there is something to be gained from the life hereafter that would be beneficial in this earthly existence. Those who feel that connection usually rely more and more on prayer in dealing with the tests and trials of life and, at times, ask for assistance from other souls who have passed on to the life hereafter.

There was a time when I myself would have dismissed the idea of seeking help from those souls who have passed on. When I was twenty-five, I took the first step toward seeking such assistance when I drew prayer into my life. Twenty-five years later while writing a biography of my father-in-law, Curtis Kelsey, I ran into what seemed to be an insolvable problem. I had very little information about his youth. Without that information I felt I couldn't produce a meaningful book. The fact that I had heard bits and pieces of stories about his youth from his children was awfully frustrating. I needed to make sure that what I had heard was authentic, and I knew that there had to have been other experiences of which my wife and her siblings were not aware.

One night after completing most of the manuscript, still unable to flesh out the earlier portions of his life, I bent over my typewriter and in desperation called out, "Help me, Curtis!"

The following evening I received a phone call from one of Curtis's close friends. He told me that he and his wife were moving to the Caribbean and wondered if I would like a carton of audiotapes of talks my father-in-law had given.

Four days later the carton arrived. The first tape I picked out of the box dealt primarily with my father-in-law's childhood, which included a number of fascinating experiences during his teenage years and early twenties.

I am convinced that Curtis had heard my desperate call and that the series of events I experienced after that call was no accident. As a result, I have, from time to time, sought help from others who have passed on.

11

THE ONENESS OF HUMANITY

In his role as a Spiritual Guide and Divine Educator, one of Bahá'u'lláh's responsibilities was to help people recognize falsehoods that they have embraced as the truth, expose them to what is really true, and inspire them to internalize and share these truths wisely with others, just as a competent and humble physician helps heal the sick.

Bahá'u'lláh called for everyone to abandon their prejudices and to open their eyes to what God has always known about humanity—that there is only one race, the human race, and that all six billion human beings are God's children. However, the way that people have behaved toward one another throughout the ages is proof that humanity has not grasped this reality.

Bahá'u'lláh's powerful proclamation of the oneness of humankind clashes with the view to which many people still cling—the belief that there are distinct and separate races and that there are those who are inherently inferior and those who are inherently superior. Eminent scientists, philosophers, and religious leaders of the past have promulgated these notions as truths, and many people, including some educators, wholeheartedly embraced them. These deeply rooted prejudices have evolved into full-blown racism.

Nevertheless Bahá'u'lláh's call remains current, steady, and strong. He proclaims that the oneness of humankind is a reality—a principle that existed even before the appearance of the first Homo sapiens. The following verse from Bahá'u'lláh's *Hidden Words* indicates that this principle has always existed in the mind of God: "Veiled in My immemorial being and in the ancient eternity of My essence, I knew My love for thee; therefore I created thee, have engraved on thee Mine image and revealed to thee My beauty."[1] This means that all six billion humans were created in the image and likeness of God.

From the outset humans have been related, belonging to the same species. While biologically we are at least fiftieth cousins, in reality we are actually closer than that. We are souls who are connected to the same Supreme Parent, making everyone on our planet, regardless of geographical location, ethnicity, religion, or culture, spiritual brothers and sisters. This reality was as true in ancient Africa, Asia, Europe, and the Americas as it is today. But ignorance, superstition, and erroneous scientific and religious beliefs have kept people from recognizing the oneness of humankind. Bahá'u'lláh endured more than forty years of exile and persecution in order to alert humanity to this fundamental reality. He also revealed ways to overcome the barriers to unity and to internalize oneness. He did this during a time when even the most learned individuals in the world possessed a fractured view of humanity, believing and inculcating the idea that there are four separate and distinct races—black, white, yellow, and red—and the notion that different ethnic groups were innately suspicious and hostile toward one another. Despite the extensive social, economic, political, and religious fragmentation and feuding in his day, Bahá'u'lláh's mission remained constant. Not even the numerous personal attacks and harsh treatment he experienced in prison deterred him. He continually reminded humanity that all people are the children of God and are therefore members of the same race—the human race. He put it this way: "Ye are the fruits of one tree, and the leaves of one branch. Deal ye one with another with the utmost love and harmony, with friendliness and fellowship. . . . So powerful is the light of unity that it can illuminate the whole earth."[2]

The oneness of humankind is not some optimist's pipe dream, nor is it merely a well-reasoned concept or theory. It is a legitimate principle. Principles, after all, are the fundamental laws upon which a body of scientific knowledge rests. They are operating in the world of nature regardless of whether we are aware of them. Take gravity, for example. Gravity, which is a principle of physics, was in operation long before an apple fell on Isaac Newton's head. Objects in the physical universe have always behaved according to the principle of gravity despite the multitude of old and often outlandish theories that were once postulated to explain their behavior.

The laws and principles that govern the creation are discovered through the observation of phenomena and are not created by invention. They are fundamental truths—guidelines that enable us to understand human nature, help us to discover and develop our true selves, and empower us to protect and preserve our planet. When we understand and live in harmony with these principles, life becomes a more manageable and fulfilling experience. Life would be rather difficult if we did not understand the principle of gravity. By the same token, life for human beings has been made difficult because of our long history of ignorance of the principle of the oneness of humankind.

It is impossible to quantify the carnage and suffering that could have been avoided if humanity had recognized and internalized the principle of oneness. There would have been no Inquisition, no holy crusades or world wars, no genocide staining human history and leaving people today skeptical about the possibility of achieving true world peace. Yet despite our skepticism Bahá'u'lláh insists that it is only a matter of time before humanity will recognize and embrace its oneness and, as a result, establish a universal and lasting peace.

There are already some signs of progress that give us reason to be hopeful. We are in the midst of a great paradigm shift, driven by Bahá'u'lláh's nineteenth-century call, in which the scientific community has denounced belief in the separateness of races. For example, Yale University biologist Jonathan Marks states, "'Race has no basic biological reality.'"[3] Many scientists now recognize the oneness of humankind as a fundamental principle of life, and not just as a recent evolutionary development but as a reality that has always existed.

Enlightened scientists such as anthropologist John Ladd of Brown University recognize that modern science must be forthcoming and admit that the scientific community has been responsible for misleading humanity by spreading the theory that there were a number of races, some superior to others: "'We the researchers are taking action to correct a legacy of misconception about the biology of race in which earlier generations of researchers provided the raw material for serious claims of racial superiority. They liked to concoct a biological basis for mistreating people.'"[4]

Anthropologist Leonard Lieberman of Central Michigan University asserts, "'Misconceptions about race have led to forms of racism that have caused much social, psychological and physical harm. These misconceptions have their origin in various papers and books that depend heavily on old and outmoded biological concepts of race.'" According to a statement of the American Anthropological Association, "'differentiating species into biologically defined 'races' has proven meaningless and unscientific as a way of explaining variation, whether in intelligence or other traits.'" And anthropologist Ashley Montagu calls race "'man's most dangerous myth.'"[5]

To set straight the record on race, the world's leading geneticists, anthropologists, paleontologists, sociologists, and social psychologists came together in Vienna, Austria, in 1995 to assess the scientific validity of the concept of race. Summarizing their scholarly discussions, anthropologist Lionel Tiger wrote: "The fact is that all of contemporary population genetics and molecular biology underscores that the 19th century notion of races as discrete and different entities is false. There is only gradual genetic diversity between groups. We all merge smoothly into each other. Nearly all the physically observable differences reflect very limited local adaptations to climate and other specific environmental conditions."[6]

Bahá'ís see the scientific community's recent recognition of the oneness of humankind not as a vindication of Bahá'u'lláh's position but rather as an awakening to a divine principle. They see this recognition as a cause for celebration, a sign of our collective rebirth, and a meaningful step toward fulfilling the ancient divine promise of the unification of the human family. As a result, an avalanche of commentary based on the findings of scientific studies has poured forth. Books and articles on the principle of the oneness of humankind have been made available to the public. For example, in *The Biology of Race,* Dr. James King writes, "'Since all human beings are of one species and since all populations tend to merge when they exist in contact, group differentiation will be based on cultural behavior and not on genetic differences.'" Dr. Luigi Luca Cavalli-Sforza, a Stanford Medical School scholar and one of the world's leading geneticists, has compiled a definitive atlas of the genetic profiles of over 1,800 population groups around the world. His *History and Geography of Human Genes* is the most comprehensive survey of human genetic variation ever compiled; in another book he writes, "'The difference[s] between races are . . . very limited. . . .

[T]he genes that react to climate are those that influence *external features. . . . It is because they are external that [they] strike us so forcibly, and we automatically assume that differences of similar magnitude exist below the surface. . . . This is simply not so: the remainder of our genetic make-up hardly differs at all.*'"[7]

Geneticists estimate that the variations of genetic makeup regarding what is commonly known as racial differences occupy only about one-hundredth of a percent of our genes. The differences are a simple matter of adaptation to one's environment. Our primitive ancestors' genes were programmed to produce dark skin because the first Homo sapiens emerged in Africa. Their skin pigment protected them from the tropical sun's ultraviolet rays, which we now know can cause skin cancer. On the flip side of the genetic dice, some of the migrants to the continent of Europe had a variant gene that gave them a lighter skin color. Because of their diet and their resistance to disease, these people tended to live longer and have more children, who in turn passed the trait on to their descendants. The trend continued for generations, eventually producing fair-skinned Europeans. But change of skin color in an ethnic group does not require a supernatural act; it is a natural phenomenon. According to the University of Florida anthropologist Jonathan Moore, "'skin color genes are turned off and on and very quickly in evolution. People can go from black to white, or white to black, in 10,000 years.'"[8]

Dr. J. Craig Venter, head of the Celera Genomics Corporation in Rockville, Maryland, and scientists at the National Institutes of Health announced that they have put together a draft of the entire sequence of the human genome, and the researchers have unanimously declared there is only one race—the human race. Thus it has been proven scientifically that people living in Africa, the Arctic, Asia, Europe, the Americas, and the Pacific are, although superficially different, actually one.

Once we accept what science has already determined to be true, human society can move beyond obsolete notions of separateness and unite. But this will not be a simple process. To understand intellectually that we are in fact one human race is one thing. To act on that understanding and change our behavior accordingly is another. Chapter 12 examines this process of transformation and shares some personal experiences related to it.

12
EMBRACING ONENESS

There are approximately six million Bahá'ís living in virtually every corner of the globe. They have embraced the principle of the oneness of humankind and are working to help set off the fire of spiritual transformation that will eventually envelop our planet. Imagine all of humanity freed from the misguided notion that there are different races and freed from all prejudices. Imagine them instead viewing everyone they meet, regardless of ethnicity or nationality, as a family member. Bahá'ís today have a sense of what that world would be like. When they look within their own spiritual communities they see themselves as part of a social dynamic that is striving to transcend the barriers that keep people apart.

Bahá'ís see Arab and Jew, Albanian and Serb, Hutu and Tutsi, Turk and Kurd, black and white, Indian and Pakistani, Irish Catholic and Protestant as possessing a common link with God. They are optimistic about the future and believe that a change of heart can happen because they have personally experienced it and know of others who have as well.

They believe it is possible for anyone to change and find the good and peace within themselves. With this outlook, they strive to become forces of unity in their communities.

From the time I embraced the Bahá'í Faith, I felt it was my responsibility to understand and internalize the central teaching of the Faith—the oneness of humankind. I thought I had some awareness of the principle, but after reading an appeal that Bahá'u'lláh's eldest son, 'Abdu'l-Bahá, made to an audience in Boston in 1912, I soon discovered that I had, in fact, a very limited understanding. 'Abdu'l-Bahá's deceptively simple appeal was "seek the realities underlying the oneness of the world of humanity."[1]

Not knowing what those underlying realities were, I embarked on a serious search for them. I began to study the scientific and spiritual proofs of oneness. What I learned boggled my mind and unshackled me from the ideas I was raised to believe were true. But it wasn't easy to let go of what I had been raised to believe. I found myself emotionally attached to falsehoods that I had long assumed were truths. It seemed as if everyone I had ever known believed that there were different races, but the Bahá'í Faith taught that there is only one race—the human race.

At first it seemed that by embracing Bahá'u'lláh's teaching that there is only one race I was going against the social grain. In fact, my friends initially rejected this idea of oneness. However, those same friends were later impressed with evidence I found to support my new belief. I found it in the concept of breathing. My friends and I marveled over the idea that breathing is an invisible chain that biologically links all human beings.

It is estimated that humans take approximately thirty thousand breaths daily. With each breath, we inhale and exhale trillions of atoms, the fundamental building block of all matter. Without atoms there cannot be molecules, without molecules we cannot have cells, without cells there can be no tissue, without tissue we have no organs, and without organs humans cannot exist. Every time we exhale, we are releasing pieces of our brain cells, heart cells, and DNA, and those who are sitting next to us, regardless of their ethnicity, are absorbing them. Outside, components of our own bodies are being swept away by the winds to faraway places where people of other nations and ethnicities absorb them, and vice versa. This interchange of atoms has been going on ever since life originated on our planet.

I also discovered that breeding between different ethnic groups is proof that we are all members of the same race. A Ghanaian from Africa and a Swede from Europe can produce a child, but a human and a gorilla cannot.

Two different species cannot produce viable offspring together. There are superficial differences among humans, just as there are variations within plant or animal species, but that does not mean we are different races. Though we are members of the same human family, each human being has his or her own individuality. This is the principle of unity in diversity, which operates at every level of nature.

An example of this principle can be seen in the structure of the human body. Though the heart, lungs, pancreas, liver, stomach, and kidneys have various functions, they must operate harmoniously to keep the body in good physical health. Each is an essential part that contributes to the whole. Separately, the organs have no value, but together they give us life. This relationship between the organs and the body is much like the relationship between the individual and society. If one organ isn't functioning optimally, it affects the entire body. The Bahá'í writings express this principle in relation to the individual and society, saying, "We belong to an organic unit and when one part of the organism suffers all the rest of the body will feel its consequence."[2]

As I studied Bahá'í scripture, I encountered an explanation of the term "children of God." The following exhortation opened my eyes to how close we truly are to one another: "Consort together in brotherly love, be ready to lay down your lives one for the other, and not only for those who are dear to you, but for all humanity. Look upon the whole human race as members of one family, all children of God; and, in so doing, you will see no difference between them."[3] The idea that every human soul is connected to God changed my attitude toward people, even those with whom I had serious differences. Over time I became far more forgiving and learned to see the good in others.

Once I embraced the principle of the oneness of humankind, I found myself wanting to draw people together, and I began to derive great pleasure from doing so. Through studying the teachings of Bahá'u'lláh, I learned the difference between oneness and unity. Oneness is a principle, a fundamental truth, whereas unity is a process. The seeds of unity are inherent in oneness. Once we internalize the principle of the oneness of humanity, we develop a natural desire to draw people together. We automatically become a force of unity wherever we may be—at home, at work, at school, and even at play.

In my search I also discovered that, like other Americans, I, too, had been affected by racism, which, the Bahá'í teachings point out, is a powerfully divisive part of American culture: "As to racial prejudice, the corrosion of which, for well-nigh a century, has bitten into the fiber, and attacked the whole social structure of American society, it should be regarded as constituting the most vital and challenging issue. . . ."[4] Before I could truly internalize the reality that everyone is my brother or sister, I had to acknowledge the possibility that I harbored some racial prejudice. During some serious soul searching, I experienced a major breakthrough when I first realized that I, too, had racist tendencies.

The incident that helped me realize I had racist tendencies occurred during my early twenties, before I learned about the Bahá'í Faith. I was driving on a busy expressway, eager to arrive on time for a work-related appointment. The driver ahead of me was plodding along at forty miles per hour, and I knew that if I continued at that pace I would be late for my appointment with a potential client. Heavy traffic made it impossible for me to pass the creeping car ahead of me. Furious, I pressed on the horn. But that seemed to have no effect. Wanting to see who the driver was so I could cuss him out, I arched over the steering wheel and peered through the windshield. The driver turned around to see who was tailgating his car. He was an elderly black man. The words "Move, nigger!" instantly flashed through my mind. Anger and hatred toward a person I didn't even know welled up in my heart.

I was horrified to realize that I could think and feel that way. After all, I had always thought of myself as a champion for minorities. Disturbed by my behavior, I thought to myself, I didn't choose to think and feel this way. Where did these thoughts come from? I wondered in horror. I was so ashamed of myself that I forgot about making the appointment on time. I didn't care that I was still plodding along slowly, because I was facing an issue that was far more important than securing a sale. I wanted to find a way to stop the car in front of me so I could apologize to the driver. But that was impossible.

Attempting to redeem myself, an inner voice started to list all of the wonderful things I had done in the field of human rights. I told myself that all of the work I had done to help people certainly outweighed my conduct on the road. I promised myself that I would never behave that way again. It was a vow I was certain I would keep.

But I was wrong. I experienced other emotional racial encounters, which I quickly tried to ignore and forget. I actually became quite skillful at repressing those episodes. Maintaining my pro-human rights image was my primary concern. But when I began attending Bahá'í meetings I developed the courage to come to grips with my infection with the disease of racism. At these gatherings I met diverse people—people of different skin colors, ages, cultures, religions, ethnicities, and temperaments—who were sincerely trying to love and understand one another and overcome their character flaws and prejudices. This gave me hope. Seeing Bahá'ís making genuine progress at unity kept me going in my quest to eliminate my prejudices.

Although becoming a Bahá'í did not free me of my infection with racism, it did compel me to work at overcoming the malady. To Bahá'ís, overcoming one's prejudices is a spiritual responsibility. I found myself engaged in a transformational process. The more headway I made in healing the infection the more progress I made at internalizing the oneness of humankind. It has been a liberating experience.

Overcoming a disease, even one as corrosive as racism, requires continued effort and diligence. Bahá'ís believe that turning to God for His help in freeing ourselves of the poison of racial prejudice, embracing our oneness, and working to create unity wherever we may be are of paramount importance at this time in the life of humanity. Once we recognize and accept the ways that racism and its harmful effects have infected our own lives, we can begin to purge it from our hearts and make real progress.

13
TIMES OF CHANGE

It can be difficult to maintain a sense of optimism about the future. For one thing, we must overcome the negative outlook of friends and acquaintances whose attitudes are easily supported by a constant flow of bad news. Even if we are idealistic, we may know only a few of the steps that are needed to bring about a better world for ourselves, our families, and our communities. We may struggle with our own natural inertia. Where can we find enough like-minded people to make a difference in the world? How can we keep from losing faith? And where can we find a complete vision for the future? Our own will always falls short. We need a vision that is acceptable to many people, a vision that everyone can help to realize.

The Bahá'í Faith provides a vision for the future that approximately six million people worldwide are working together to realize. It describes a glorious, hopeful future while also recognizing that a period of intense suffering may precede it. Consider the process a woman goes through in childbirth; it can be extremely painful, but the result is extremely worthwhile.

Not only is the Bahá'í vision encouraging to those who have almost lost hope, but it offers guidance on how to transform ourselves spiritually into caring, loving beings who are committed to creating that future.

Bahá'u'lláh's mission is to enable people to recognize and accept that "The earth is but one country, and mankind its citizens." By understanding that we are all brothers and sisters, we are moved to work together to take responsibility for our collective future. True spiritual transformation of the individual, the family, the community, and the world requires religion, for it links us with our Creator and provides us with divine guidance. Bahá'u'lláh asserts that "Religion is the greatest of all means for the establishment of order in the world and for the peaceful contentment of all that dwell therein."[1]

The Bahá'í Faith teaches that individuals can achieve great potential and that the challenging but hopeful changes occurring around the world are enabling man to reveal "the full measure of his destiny on earth, the innate excellence of his reality."[2] At the core of Bahá'u'lláh's revelation are principles to guide humanity to the next level of its development, from its adolescence to its maturity. These principles include, among others, the elimination of all forms of prejudice, the equality of women and men, the harmony of science and religion, and universal education. These are principles that Bahá'ís are advocating and attempting to practice in their own lives every day. Fortified with Bahá'u'lláh's guidance, Bahá'ís are confident that unity can and will be achieved.

Bahá'u'lláh's vision calls for the realization of what men and women everywhere have longed, prayed, fought, and appealed for throughout the centuries. It has stimulated change in many hearts and has helped people marshal the courage to see what has been revealed to us—a divine response to our pleas for help.

Bahá'u'lláh tells us that we are living in a special period of history and that the world's destiny is unimaginably glorious: "The Call of God, when raised, breathed a new life into the body of mankind, and infused a new spirit into the whole creation. It is for this reason that the world hath been moved to its depths, and the hearts and consciences . . . been quickened. Erelong the evidences of this regeneration will be revealed, and the fast asleep will be awakened."[3]

Bahá'u'lláh's proclamation that he is the Spiritual Guide, the Divine Educator for this day and age, unleashed a mighty gale of change that is still sweeping across our planet. It will continue to do so until his vision is at last made real. This day is a time of great hope and fulfillment as well as a time of upheaval.

Tremors of change are being felt everywhere, from Papua New Guinea to Iceland, from Sri Lanka to Chile, and from the Aleutian Islands to the Solomons. It does not matter how isolated a country may seem, how provincial a people may be, or what kind of government may rule a nation, all parts of the world have been, and continue to be, moved by Bahá'u'lláh's vibrating message.

At the time of Bahá'u'lláh's revelation in the mid-1800s, there was a sense of finality about human development and achievement that pervaded many circles of authority. The U.S. Congress, for example, was seriously thinking of closing the government's patent office because it was widely believed that everything that needed to be invented had already been created. Virtually every area of the world had been explored. Christianity had been preached in every part of the planet. Those in power seemed firmly entrenched in their ruling positions.

However, in the face of all of this, a voice cried out from the Middle East, asking humanity to put aside its differences and unite to build the kingdom of God on earth.

The nineteenth century was a time when many mighty thrones buckled and eventually toppled. Revolutions broke out in lands that had once seemed invulnerable to political change. Workers rebelled against factory owners, peasants demanded their freedom from feudal lords, the disenfranchised rose up against the establishment, women clamored for equality with men, and civil rights movements mushroomed all around the planet. While religion waned, materialistic ideologies promoting the self, political truths, or scientific truths captured peoples' imaginations, drawing their attention away from the need for spiritual growth. A planetary purging had been launched, its intensity increasing with every passing day, heightening confusion and suspicion everywhere. This process continued and even accelerated throughout the twentieth century.

Amid the chaos, suffering, and inner pain that the disintegration of the present world is generating, a new spirit is rising. This new spirit is raising people's social awareness and inspiring broader, deeper thinking. An unprecedented surge of optimism among scientists is driving them to probe, discover, and create more, for their yearning to unravel life's secrets seems boundless.

This burst of creative energy has enabled some people in different parts of the world to recognize aspects of reality of which past generations were unaware. Natural barriers have been transcended by technological advancements, allowing former enemies to communicate with one another and overcome ancient prejudices. Today more and more of us are beginning to view the earth as a single homeland for all people, sensing that all of its inhabitants are somehow related. A new level of world consciousness seems to be spreading everywhere. Those who are attuned to this new spirit view the internationalization of our planet as inevitable. Nations that were once bitter foes are abandoning old animosities and sharing resources so that their citizens can enjoy better lives. When disaster strikes one part of the world, it sparks a speedy response in nearly every other part of the world.

The world is undergoing a transition that is similar in essence to previous times of great change but unique in scope and magnitude. As humanity moves through this unsettling period, the big questions are: Where is all this change leading? What is causing the unifying impulse that is at work in the world today? And what can I, as an individual, do to promote positive change in my life, in my family's life, and in the world?

14
A UNIFIED WORLD

Bahá'u'lláh gave guidance for personal spiritual growth and established a plan for creating a unified world society whose time has come. Over one hundred years ago, through Bahá'u'lláh's writings and teachings, God expressed what humanity needs to do to fulfill the words of the Lord's Prayer, "Thy kingdom come. Thy will be done in earth, as it is in heaven."[1]

The logical next step in humanity's social evolution is planetary unification. The journey we have taken to reach this point has been long, arduous, and often bloody. The process of civilizing human character has been uneven and has not been equitable to all in the material benefits it has brought. First we had to achieve unity at the level of the family, and then we had to learn how to unify ourselves at the level of the tribe. Then emerged the city-state, which eventually gave rise to the nation. The physical unification of the planet through the elimination of physical and technological barriers that once separated the peoples of the world from one another is accomplished, and the interdependence of all who inhabit the earth is acknowledged. We stand at the threshold of the next stage in the advancement of civilization; humanity is experiencing its collective coming of age. The Bahá'í writings explain,

> Unification of the whole of mankind is the hall-mark of the stage which human society is now approaching. Unity of family, of tribe, of city-state, and nation have been successively attempted and fully established. World unity is the goal towards which a harassed humanity is striving. Nation-building has come to an end. The anarchy inherent in state sovereignty is moving towards a climax. A world, growing to maturity, must abandon this fetish, recognize the oneness and wholeness of human relationships, and establish once for all the machinery that can best incarnate this fundamental principle of its life.[2]

Naturally there is resistance, just as there was during the period of history when families feuded and it seemed impossible for them to unite into a tribe. For hundreds of years tribes battered and bloodied each other, but eventually they came together to form city-states. The formation of nations followed a similar pattern as warring city-states eventually banded together to form nations. For hundreds of years nations have been battling and distrusting each other. But in time the nations will, of necessity, forge a planetary union that is the result of a new, unified relationship; however, this will not happen before we have had to endure severe hardships that force us to take this next step in humanity's development. As mentioned, taking the next step in our development is like giving birth to a child. Just as a mother, despite the agony of labor, experiences joy when she finally sees her baby, so, too, will humanity celebrate the fruits of its labor after enduring great tribulations. Bahá'u'lláh writes, "'The whole earth is now in a state of pregnancy. The day is approaching when it will have yielded its noblest fruits, when from it will have sprung forth the loftiest trees, the most enchanting blossoms, the most heavenly blessings.'"[3]

A better world will slowly and steadily emerge as more people become aware of the divine process that is driving humanity, despite its resistance, toward unity and harmony. This inviolable, irresistible movement toward world unity was initiated by Bahá'u'lláh in 1863 when he declared that he was a prophet from God and that it is God's will for the human race to be united.

Evidence that this movement toward unity is alive is growing ever more discernible. In the latter part of the twentieth century the Cold War came to an abrupt end, stunning the most eminent geopolitical pundits, who had predicted a long and protracted struggle. Soviet communism died, and the United States welcomed Russia into the fold of democratic nations. A growing free-market economy is flourishing in China. Ancient national feuds are, of necessity, ending. France and Germany, longtime battlefield adversaries, are partners in the expanding European Union, which is developing into a political entity as well as a powerful economic force known as the European Community. National tariffs no longer exist in the Union. Everyone living in the member nations carries the same European Union passport. The Union has its own currency, the Euro. A European Union armed forces is being developed. Even the United Kingdom, which for centuries considered itself separate from Europe, has joined the compact.

The pull toward unification is being felt elsewhere, too. In Southeast Asia, for example, Thailand, Malaysia, Singapore, the Philippines, Brunei, Vietnam, and Indonesia have formed a common-market-like union. A number of South American nations are working on developing a similar union in their part of the world. The World Trade Organization has been established and is accelerating the free flow of goods between most nations in the world. The idea of an international collective security force became a reality when scores of nations, under the banner of the United Nations, pushed back the Iraqi invasion of Kuwait during the Persian Gulf War of 1990–91. Similar armed international interventions have been used in recent years to halt violence in such places as Bosnia, Kosovo, and East Timor. The value of upholding and defending human rights is gaining ascendance over the concern for maintaining national sovereignty. Efforts are being made to create an international police force, sponsored by the United Nations, that will be equipped to put down the land-grabbing initiatives of regional tyrants.

The pull toward unity is also apparent in the ways that we are tackling crises. When famine ravaged Ethiopia, for example, scores of nations rushed food and medicine to the stricken nation. The same was true when India and El Salvador were struck by deadly earthquakes. An international spirit of empathy has developed. Women's rights are being recognized increasingly in all parts of the world, leading to greater opportunities for work and a greater measure of influence in government affairs. The United Kingdom, India, Sri Lanka, Pakistan, and Israel have all had women serving as prime ministers.

Businesses have expanded beyond their national borders. Many American corporations, for example, now have interests and operations throughout the world. Many Japanese car manufacturers are building vehicles in the United States. Companies are entering into international joint ventures. Nations are combining their scientific expertise to develop new technologies. An international space station, the result of cooperation between sixteen countries, recently began operation in Earth's orbit.

New medicines are being shared worldwide. Through the use of satellites, television, and the Internet, surgical techniques can be witnessed simultaneously in disparate locations around the world. Robots are being used to perform certain surgical procedures. New drugs have been invented that free men and women from languishing in prison-like mental hospitals and allow them to lead productive lives.

This scientific explosion is helping to further Bahá'u'lláh's call for the unification of our planet. People who were once cut off from one another by natural barriers are now linked to one another by modern communications networks. Children in different parts of the world can communicate with each other by E-mail, and a university education can be accessed through one's computer.

Furthermore, scientists and religionists are beginning to appreciate each other's pursuits more fully and are beginning to see the need for an ongoing, deepening dialogue between science and religion. Albert Einstein articulated the need for science and religion to work in harmony, saying, "Science without religion is lame, religion without science is blind."[4]

Since the time of Bahá'u'lláh's ministry there has been an increase in the liberation of subjugated peoples. The institutions of Russian serfdom and American slavery were both ended. Colonialism has been virtually eliminated. Racism is being exposed, and collective efforts are being made to uproot it from society. Throughout the world, pressure to stop racist practices is being applied to governments that promote or condone racism. Child labor has been abolished in many parts of the world. In several countries where it was not previously the case, the average worker is now earning a livable wage. Governments are growing increasingly aware of the importance of caring for the disabled and the elderly, and some are providing free medical treatment and education for their citizens. Class prejudice is being actively attacked. There is worldwide interest and involvement in human rights struggles around the globe. Organizations such as Amnesty International, with its worldwide membership, have sprung up to oppose and raise awareness of human rights violations. Religious persecution in many places has aroused concern among governments and individuals around the world, and protests to various international agencies have been lodged on behalf of beleaguered religious minorities.

Because of this growing world consciousness, a government's act of oppression against one of its minorities is becoming less likely to go undetected. A collective impulse to correct wrongdoings seems to be emerging. The next step will be the creation of an international organization that can end repression as well as improve everyone's quality of life. There are no precedents for creating a global society and establishing world peace. Although almost all of the necessary technology has been developed, something more is clearly needed.

Since the mid-1800s remarkable progress has been made in establishing such an international organization. First the League of Nations was established in 1919 after World War I. Though the league ultimately collapsed during World War II, it succeeded nonetheless in awakening humanity to the need for a similar but stronger organization. After World War II, on 24 October 1945, the United Nations was established to "promote respect for human rights, protect the environment, fight disease, foster development and reduce poverty."[5] Now other international agencies have been formed to clean up the skies, waterways, and land,

and to improve farming methods, especially in the less developed areas of the world.

While phenomenal, systemic changes are occurring on a worldwide scale, people throughout the world are overcoming their seemingly insurmountable differences with one another: Where there was once hate, love has bloomed; where unspeakable acts of violence were perpetrated, forgiveness has been forthcoming; and where there were once impenetrable barriers to unity and common purpose, peace has sprung up. These things are happening within the Bahá'í community, and those who witness them are stunned by what they observe. Some say it is miraculous.

In thousands of localities—from villages north of the Arctic Circle to territories near Antarctica, and even in the Amazon jungle—Bahá'ís are working to create communities in which everyone is recognized as a child of God, everyone is developing a global perspective, everyone is working to accept and love one another, and everyone is working to rid himself or herself of all prejudices. Within these communities people of different ages, skin colors, nationalities, religious backgrounds, and personalities are striving to live together in unity. By relying on Bahá'u'lláh's teachings to guide their efforts, Bahá'ís are making remarkable progress in developing a cohesive spirit of family and are drawing ever closer to that time when the oneness of humanity will be realized.

It is a struggle. It is tough to unlearn lessons that we were taught as children and have believed for many years to be true, but it is happening little by little. The process demands effort on the part of everyone, as well as courage, optimism, and love for each other. Every person has the potential to achieve this, for the Bahá'í writings assert that "The potentialities inherent in the station of man, the full measure of his destiny on earth, the innate excellence of his reality, must all be manifested in this promised Day of God."[6] The spiritual development in which every single Bahá'í is engaged is important because all are helping to establish a pattern for a world civilization that will one day be free of the anguish and torment that plague humanity today. Bahá'u'lláh's vision sustains Bahá'ís and inspires them to forge ahead with putting into practice what is needed to establish a world civilization that recognizes and treats all people as children of God.

In the search for faith and meaning, we may travel many different paths, but we can be confident that the true path for our own spiritual growth and for the advancement of civilization will be made clear. To sincere and earnest seekers of faith, Bahá'u'lláh has made the following promise: ". . . when the lamp of search, of earnest striving, of longing desire, of passionate devotion, of fervid love, of rapture and ecstasy, is kindled within the seeker's heart . . . Then will the manifold favors and outpouring grace of the holy and everlasting Spirit confer such new life upon the seeker that he will find himself endowed with a new eye, a new ear, a new heart, and a new mind. He will contemplate the manifest signs of the universe, and will penetrate the hidden mysteries of the soul."[7]

NOTES

CHAPTER 5 / THE GATE

1. The Báb, quoted in Nabíl, *Dawn-Breakers,* p. 57.

2. Mullá Ḥusayn, quoted in Nabíl, *Dawn-Breakers,* p. 65.

3. Vaḥíd, quoted in Nabíl, *Dawn-Breakers,* p. 469.

4. The Báb, quoted in Nabíl, *Dawn-Breakers,* p. 93.

5. The Báb, *Selections from the Writings of the Báb,* p. 80.

6. The Báb, quoted in Nabíl, *Dawn-Breakers,* pp. 315–16.

7. The Báb, quoted in Nabíl, *Dawn-Breakers,* p. 509.

8. The Báb, quoted in Nabíl, *Dawn-Breakers,* p. 512.

9. The Báb, quoted in Nabíl, *Dawn-Breakers,* p. 513.

10. The Báb, quoted in Nabíl, *Dawn-Breakers,* p. 514.

11. The Báb, quoted in Bahá'u'lláh, *Kitáb-i-Aqdas,* p. 245.

CHAPTER 6 / THE GLORY OF GOD

1. Shoghi Effendi, *God Passes By,* p. 101.

2. Bahá'u'lláh, *Epistle,* p. 21.

3. Bahá'u'lláh, *Epistle,* p. 22.

4. Bahá'u'lláh, quoted in Shoghi Effendi, *God Passes By,* pp. 101–02.

5. Bahá'u'lláh, *Gleanings,* pp. 6, 7.

6. Bahá'u'lláh, *Kitáb-i-Íqán,* pp. 250–51.

7. Bahá'u'lláh, *Kitáb-i-Íqán,* p. 251.

8. Bahá'u'lláh, quoted in Balyuzi, *Bahá'u'lláh,* p. 148.

9. Bahá'u'lláh, *Kitáb-i-Íqán,* pp. 195–96.

10. Bahá'u'lláh, *Hidden Words,* p. 3; ibid, Arabic, no. 1.

11. Bahá'u'lláh, *The Seven Valleys and The Four Valleys,* p. 4.

CHAPTER 7 / THE PROMISED DAY

1. Bahá'u'lláh, quoted in Shoghi Effendi, *God Passes By,* p. 147.
2. Bahá'u'lláh, *Kitáb-i-Aqdas,* para. 75.
3. Bahá'u'lláh, *Gleanings,* pp. 6, 7.
4. Bahá'u'lláh, quoted in Shoghi Effendi, *Promised Day Is Come,* paras. 43, 44–45.
5. Bahá'u'lláh, *Proclamation,* pp. 50–51.
6. Queen Victoria, quoted in Shoghi Effendi, *Promised Day Is Come,* para. 163.
7. Bahá'u'lláh, quoted in Shoghi Effendi, *God Passes By,* p. 187.
8. Bahá'u'lláh, *Proclamation,* pp. 83, 84.
9. Bahá'u'lláh, quoted in Shoghi Effendi, *God Passes By,* p. 278.
10. E. G. Browne, quoted in Balyuzi, *Bahá'u'lláh,* pp. 372–73.

CHAPTER 8 / OUR SPIRITUAL REALITY

1. Bahá'u'lláh, *Gleanings,* p. 285.
2. Bahá'u'lláh, *Epistle,* p. 79; Bahá'u'lláh, in *Bahá'í Prayers,* pp. 211–12.
3. Bahá'u'lláh, *Gleanings,* p. 185; Bahá'u'lláh, *Hidden Words,* Arabic, no. 13.
4. Matthew 6:9–13 (KJV).
5. Bahá'u'lláh, *Hidden Words,* Arabic, no. 5.
6. Extract from a letter written on behalf of Shoghi Effendi, quoted in *Messages from the Universal House of Justice, 1963–1986,* 211:3a.

CHAPTER 9 / THE PURPOSE OF LIFE

1. Bahá'u'lláh, in *Bahá'í Prayers,* p. 4.

CHAPTER 10 / THE SOUL'S JOURNEY

1. Horace Holley, *Religion for Mankind,* p. 193.

CHAPTER 11 / THE ONENESS OF HUMANITY

1. Bahá'u'lláh, *Hidden Words,* Arabic, no. 3.
2. Bahá'u'lláh, *Epistle,* p. 14.
3. Jonathan Marks, quoted in *The Power of Race Unity,* p. 33.
4. John Ladd, quoted in *The Power of Race Unity,* p. 33.
5. Leonard Lieberman, quoted in *The Power of Race Unity,* p. 33; the American Anthropological Association, statement quoted in ibid; Ashley Montagu, quoted in ibid.
6. Lionel Tiger, "Trump the Race Card," *Wall Street Journal,* 23 Feb. 1996.
7. James C. King, quoted in *The Power of Race Unity,* p. 34; Luigi Luca Cavalli-Sforza, quoted in ibid.
8. Jonathan Moore, quoted in *The Power of Race Unity,* p. 35.

CHAPTER 12 / EMBRACING ONENESS

1. 'Abdu'l-Bahá, *Promulgation of Universal Peace,* p. 144.
2. Extract from a letter dated 14 April 1932 written on behalf of Shoghi Effendi to a Bahá'í family, in *Lights of Guidance,* p. 133, no. 446.
3. 'Abdu'l-Bahá, *Paris Talks,* 53:11.
4. Shoghi Effendi, *Advent of Divine Justice,* p. 33.

CHAPTER 13 / TIMES OF CHANGE

1. Bahá'u'lláh, *Gleanings,* p. 250; Bahá'u'lláh, quoted in Shoghi Effendi, *World Order of Baha'u'llah,* p. 186
2. Bahá'u'lláh, *Gleanings,* p. 340.
3. Bahá'u'lláh, quoted in Shoghi Effendi, *World Order of Baha'u'llah,* p. 169.

CHAPTER 14 / A UNIFIED WORLD

1. Matthew 6:10 (KJV).

2. Shoghi Effendi, *World Order of Bahá'u'lláh,* p. 202.

3. Bahá'u'lláh, quoted in Shoghi Effendi, *World Order of Bahá'u'lláh,* p. 169.

4. Albert Einstein, quoted in Guy Murchie, *Seven Mysteries of Life,* p. 615.

5. http://www.un.org/Overviewbrief.html.

6. Bahá'u'lláh, *Gleanings,* p. 340.

7. Bahá'u'lláh, *Gleanings,* p. 267.

BIBLIOGRAPHY

WORKS OF BAHÁ'U'LLÁH

Epistle to the Son of the Wolf. Translated by Shoghi Effendi. 1st pocket-size ed. Wilmette, Ill.: Bahá'í Publishing Trust, 1988.

Gleanings from the Writings of Bahá'u'lláh. Translated by Shoghi Effendi. 1st pocket-size ed. Wilmette, Ill.: Bahá'í Publishing Trust, 1983.

The Hidden Words. Translated by Shoghi Effendi. Wilmette, Ill.: Bahá'í Publishing Trust, 1939.

The Kitáb-i-Aqdas: The Most Holy Book. 1st pocket-size ed. Wilmette, Ill: Bahá'í Publishing Trust, 1993.

The Kitáb-i-Íqán: The Book of Certitude. 1st pocket-size ed. Translated by Shoghi Effendi. Wilmette, Ill.: Bahá'í Publishing Trust, 1983.

The Proclamation of Bahá'u'lláh to the Kings and Leaders of the World. Haifa: Bahá'í World Centre, 1972.

The Seven Valleys and The Four Valleys. New ed. Translated by Marzieh Gail and Ali-Kuli Khan. Wilmette, Ill.: Bahá'í Publishing Trust, 1991.

WORKS OF THE BÁB

Selections from the Writings of the Báb. Compiled by the Research Department of the Universal House of Justice. Translated by Habib Taherzadeh et al. Haifa: Bahá'í World Centre, 1976.

WORKS OF 'ABDU'L-BAHÁ

Paris Talks: Addresses Given by 'Abdu'l-Bahá in 1911. 12th ed. London: Bahá'í Publishing Trust, 1995.

The Promulgation of Universal Peace: Talks Delivered by 'Abdu'l-Bahá during His Visit to the United States and Canada in 1912. Compiled by Howard MacNutt. 2d ed. Wilmette, Ill.: Bahá'í Publishing Trust, 1982.

OTHER WORKS

Bahá'u'lláh, the Báb, and 'Abdu'l-Bahá. *Bahá'í Prayers: A Selection of Prayers Revealed by Bahá'u'lláh, the Báb, and 'Abdu'l-Bahá.* New ed. Wilmette, Ill: Bahá'í Publishing Trust, 1991.

Balyuzi, H. M. *Bahá'u'lláh: The King of Glory.* Oxford: George Ronald, 1980.

Holley, Horace. *Religion for Mankind.* London: George Ronald, 1956; Wilmette, Ill.: Bahá'í Publishing Trust, 1966.

Lights of Guidance. Compiled by Helen Hornby. 6th ed. New Delhi: Bahá'í Publishing Trust, 1999.

Messages from the Universal House of Justice, 1963–1986: The Third Epoch of the Formative Age. Compiled by Geoffry W. Marks. Wilmette, Ill.: Bahá'í Publishing Trust, 1996.

Nabíl-i-A'ẓam [Muḥammad-i-Zarandí]. *The Dawn-Breakers: Nabíl's Narrative of the Early Days of the Bahá'í Revelation.* Translated and edited by Shoghi Effendi. Wilmette, Ill.: Bahá'í Publishing Trust, 1932.

The Oxford Dictionary of Quotations. 5th ed. Edited by Elizabeth Knowles. Oxford: Oxford University Press, 1999.

The Power of Race Unity: Handbook for Neighborhood Race Unity Dialogues. 1st ed. [n.p.: National Spiritual Assembly of the Bahá'ís of the United States], 1998.

Shoghi Effendi. *The Advent of Divine Justice.* 1st pocket-size ed. Wilmette, Ill.: Bahá'í Publishing Trust, 1990.

Shoghi Effendi. *God Passes By.* New ed. Wilmette, Ill.: Bahá'í Publishing Trust, 1974.

Shoghi Effendi. *The Promised Day Is Come.* 3d ed. Wilmette, Ill.: Bahá'í Publishing Trust, 1980.

Shoghi Effendi. *The World Order of Bahá'u'lláh: Selected Letters.* New ed. Wilmette, Ill.: Bahá'í Publishing Trust, 1991.

Tiger, Lionel. "Trump the Race Card," *Wall Street Journal,* 23 February 1996.

INDEX

INDEX

A

'Abdu'l-Bahá, and oneness
  of humanity, 184
Abraham, 85–86
Acre, 109–10, 112
Adrianople, 104, 108–9
'Akká, 109–10, 112
'Alí Muḥammad. *See* Báb, the
American Anthropological
  Association, 176
Amnesty International, 207
animals
  differences with humans,
    18–19, 21
  similarities with humans, 20
Auroville, 41–42
Azerbaijan, mountains of, 69

B

Báb, the
  arrest of, 68
  and correspondence with
    Bahá'u'lláh, 76
  imprisonment of, in
    mountains of Azer-
    baijan, 69
  imprisonment of, in
    Tabríz, 72
  martyrdom of, 73–75
  meeting with Mullá
    Ḥusayn, 63–65
  meeting with Vaḥíd,
    68–69
  opposition toward,
    67, 71
  persecution of followers
    of, 67, 71–72, 80
  proclamation of, 72–73
  purpose of mission of,
    70–71, 75–76, 121
  recognition of, by
    disciples, 66
  revelation of the Bayán,
    70
Bábís, 75
  Bahá'u'lláh strengthens
    community of, 90
  become Bahá'ís, 105
  persecution of, 67,
    71–72, 80
  problems in community
    of, 79, 86
  strengthening of, after the
    Báb's execution, 76
  turn to Bahá'u'lláh after
    the Báb's execution, 81
  two attempt to assassi-
    nate the shah, 80
Baghdad
  Bahá'u'lláh in, 85–87,
    88–92, 99–100
  Bahá'u'lláh proclaims
    himself in garden near,
    101
Bahá'í Faith
  community of, 13, 209–10
  embraces oneness of
    humanity, 183–84,
    189–90
  provides vision for future,
    193–94
  teachings of, 194–95
  what occurs when one
    becomes a member of,
    134
Bahá'ís, 105

Bahá'ís *(continued)*
attempt to visit Bahá'u'lláh in Acre, 112
community of, 13, 209–10
embrace oneness of humanity, 183–84, 189–90
grow united during Bahá'u'lláh's imprisonment in Acre, 111
Bahá'í scripture. *See* scripture, Bahá'í
Bahá'í writings. *See* scripture, Bahá'í
Bahá'u'lláh
in Acre, 109–10
in Adrianople, 104, 108–9
agrees to perform miracle for Muslim scholars, 90–91
arrest of, in Tehran, 80, 81
the Báb reveals name of, 76
background of, 80–81
in Baghdad, 85–87, 88–92, 99–100
in Constantinople, 99–101, 103–4
and correspondence with the Báb, 76
destiny subject to will of God, 88–89
imprisonment of, in Black Pit, 81–82, 85
interview with E. G. Browne, 115–16
mission of unity, 84, 102, 171–73, 194, 196
murder attempt on life of, 92
passing of, 116–17
proclamation of, 101–2
purpose of mission of, 117, 121
receives revelation in Black Pit, 82–83
reveals Book of Certitude, The, 92–94
reveals *Kitáb-i-Aqdas, The,* 113
reveals Seven Valleys, The, 95
settles in outskirts of Acre, 113
spreads the Báb's message, 81
strengthens Bábí community, 90
teachings of, 122–24, 194–95
transfers to house outside of Acre, 112
visits Haifa, 113–14
writes to world leaders, 105–7, 108, 110–11
Bayán, the 70
belief, the process of, 25–26
Bible, 93
Biology of Race, The, 177
Black Pit
Bahá'u'lláh imprisoned in, 81–82, 85
Bahá'u'lláh receives revelation in, 82–83
body, relationship with the soul, 131–32, 138, 146–47, 159–60, 161, 163

Book of Certitude, The, 93
brain, function of, 135
Browne, E. G., interview with Bahá'u'lláh, 115–16
Buddha
effect of teachings of, 58
and the Right Path, 39
Burning Bush, 83
businesses, expanding beyond national borders, 205–6

C

Carmelite Monastery, 114
Cavalli-Sforza, Luigi Luca, 177–78
Cave of Elijah, 114
change, times of, 196–98, 207
Christians
German Adventist, 113–14
holy crusades of, 52
and return of Jesus, 41
Cold War, 204
coming of age, humanity's, 202–3
Constantinople, 99, 100–101, 103–4

D

death
connection between body and soul, 163
seeking help from souls who have passed, 166
what happens after, 164
Divine Educators. *See* Spiritual Guides
Dove, Jesus receives revelation from, 83

E

Edict of Toleration, 114–15
Egypt, Moses' exodus from, 86
Einstein, Albert, 207

F

freedom, true, 143
free will, 160

G

garden near Baghdad, 101, 103
Garden of Riḍván, 101, 103
genes, 178–79
German Adventist Christians, 113–14
God
communication of, through Spiritual Guides, 55
connection of humans to, 132–33, 144–46, 155, 187
path to, 126–27
Golden Rule, 40
gravity, 174

H

Haifa, Bahá'u'lláh visits, 113
Ḥájí Mírzá Áqásí, 69
happiness, attainment of, 17
Hidden Words, The, 94–95
Hijaz, 67

INDEX

History and Geography of Human Genes, 177
Holley, Horace, 162
human beings
- Bahá'u'lláh's vision for, 123–24
- differences with animals, 18–19, 21
- nobility of, 127
- physical nature of, 20–21
- similarities with animals, 20
- spiritual nature of, 20
- true reality of, 131
- understanding purpose of life, 18, 125, 127–28, 144–46
- uniqueness of, 18–19

human genome, 179

I

intelligence, 23
Islamic prophecies, 62
Istanbul, 99

J

Jesus
- effect of teachings of, 49, 57
- human side of, 56
- many did not recognize, 42, 57
- receives revelation, 83
- return of, 41, 62

Jews, 41
Josh, story of internship of, 135–37

K

Kelsey, Curtis, 166–67
King, James, 177
Kitáb-i-Aqdas, The, 113
Kitáb-i-Íqán, The, 93
Koran, 70, 93
Kurdistan, mountains of, 87–88, 90

L

Ladd, John, 175–76
laws and principles, as fundamental truths, 174
League of Nations, 208
lesser peace, 108
liberation, of subjugated peoples, 207
Lieberman, Leonard, 176
life
- begins at conception, 160
- purpose of, 18, 125, 127–28, 144–46

Lord's Prayer, 128, 201
love, of self, 155

M

Maiden (of Heaven), 83–84, 87
Marks, Jonathan, 175
Mecca, Muḥammad's flight from, 86
Mehdi, story of, 148–55
Messengers of God. *See* Spiritual Guides
messianic expectations, 62
mind, as aspect of the soul, 135
Mírzá Yaḥyá, 86, 108–9

Montagu, Ashley, 176
Moore, Jonathan, 178–79
morality, 40
Morse, Samuel F. B., 61–62
Moses
effect of teachings of, 57
exodus from Egypt, 86
human side of, 54, 56
receives revelation, 83
Ten Commandments of, 39
Most Holy Book, The, 113
Mount Carmel, 113–14
Muḥammad
effect of teachings of, 39–40, 57–58
flight from Mecca, 86
human side of, 56
Mullá Ḥusayn
the Báb sends to Tehran, 67, 76, 81
describes qualities of Promised One, 64
finds Promised One, 65
meets with the Báb, 63–65
searches for Promised One, 62
travels to Shiraz, 63
Muslims, Shiite, 41

N

Newton, Isaac, 174
nineteenth century, 196

O

oneness of humanity
Bahá'ís embrace, 183–84, 189–90
Bahá'u'lláh proclaims, 171–73
and difference between unity, 187
as legitimate principle, 173–74
obstacles to recognizing, 172–73
optimism, 193, 197

P

peace, 108, 127, 208
Persian Gulf War, 205
physical nature
development of, 22
of humans and animals, 20–21
relationship with the soul, 131–32, 138, 146–47, 159–60, 161, 163
and spiritual nature, 22–23, 124, 162
political systems, divisive nature of, 33
Pope Pius IX, 110–11
progressive revelation, 48–52
Prophets of God. *See* Spiritual Guides
purpose in life, 18, 125, 127–28, 144–46

Q

Queen Victoria, 108
Qur'án, 70, 93

INDEX

R

race
- belief in separateness of, 171–72
- breeding between different ethnic groups, 185–86
- human genome proves one race, 179
- reaction of genes to environment, 178
- scientists gather in Austria to discuss, 176
- separateness of, denied by scientists, 175–79

racism
- as most challenging issue, 187–88
- Nathan Rutstein examines own tendencies toward, 188–90
- story of Mehdi, 148–55
- turning to God for freedom from, 190

religion
- current trouble with, 48
- definition of, 47
- evolution of, 48–52
- necessary to order and spiritual transformation, 194
- schisms within, 38, 47
- and science, 207
- value of, 23–24

Russian consul, and Bahá'u'lláh, 85

Rutstein, Nathan
- becomes a Bahá'í, 14
- college years, 8–10
- drafted into Army, 14
- examines own racist tendencies, 188–90
- experience when writing about Curtis Kelsey, 166–67
- family escapes to U.S., 3
- investigates Bahá'í Faith, 11–14
- lecture tour in United Kingdom, 128–31
- passion for sports, 8
- questions posed during childhood, 6
- relationship with grandmother, 7–8
- religious background, 6–7
- school years, 5
- story of Josh, 135–37
- studies oneness of humanity, 184–87

S

science and religion, 207

scripture, Bahá'í
- Book of Certitude, The, 93–94
- *Hidden Words, The,* 94–95
- *Kitáb-i-Aqdas, The,* 113
- Seven Valleys, The, 95
- wisdom and knowledge in, 14

search
- Bahá'u'lláh encourages, 93
- for new Spiritual Guide, 58

for something important, 17, 25–27
for spiritual and philosophical direction, 34–35, 42–43
September 11, 2001, 31
service, 144–46
Seven Valleys, The, 95
shah, the
attempt to assassinate, 80
commissions Vahid to investigate the Báb, 68
expels Bahá'u'lláh from Baghdad, 99
Shiite Muslims, and return of Twelfth Imam, 41
Shiraz, 62, 63, 67
Síyáh-Chál. *See* Black Pit
society
comparison of, with states of human development, 122
creating global, 208
moral decay of, 31–32
root cause of problems of, 33
treating problems of, 32–34
soul
connection with God, 132, 187
relationship with the body, 131–32, 138, 146–47, 159–60, 161, 163
stages of development of, 161–65
various notions of, 125–26
virtues latent within, 133–35, 144–46, 159
spiritual growth
through developing the soul's qualities, 160
in the life hereafter, 164
obstacles to, 147
process of, 133–34, 163
role of religion in, 23–24
Spiritual Guides promote, 57
See also spiritual nature
Spiritual Guides
Bahá'u'lláh explains role of, 93
characteristics of, 35–37, 54
God communicates through, 55
and the Golden Rule, 40
human and divine sides of, 55–56
manifesting God's will, 54
and progressive revelation, 48–52
progress resulting from, 38–40
reaction of society toward, 36–37
recognizing new, 40–42, 50, 58
relationship of, with God, 37, 53, 55
role of, in spiritual development, 22, 40
schisms following death of, 38, 47
as source of divine knowledge and love, 134
as special level of creation, 53–54

Spiritual Guides *(continued)*
as teachers of humanity, 48–50, 57
spiritual nature
connection of, with God, 133, 138–39
of human beings, 20–22, 127–28
and physical nature, 22–23, 124, 152
relationship with the body, 131–32, 138, 146–47, 159–60, 161, 163
spiritual teachers remind us of, 22
See also spiritual growth
spiritual teachers. *See* Spiritual Guides
struggle, purpose of, 162

T

Tabríz, 72, 73, 75
Ṭáhirih, 66–67
technology, 206
Tehran, 67, 76
telegraph, 61–62
Ten Commandments, 39
Tiger, Lionel, 176–77
times of change, 196–98, 207
Twelfth Imam, return of, 41

U

United Nations, 208
unity
aided by scientific explosion, 206
among nations, 203–6
and difference between oneness, 187
in diversity, 186
various levels of, 201–3
Ur, 85–86

V

Vaḥíd, 68–69
Venter, J. Craig, 179
virtues, 133–35, 144–46, 159, 161

W

women's rights, recognition of, 205
World Trade Organization, 204
writings, Bahá'í. *See* scripture, Bahá'í

ABOUT THE BAHÁ'Í FAITH

In just over one hundred years the Bahá'í Faith has grown from an obscure movement in the Middle East to the second-most widespread independent world religion after Christianity. With some 5 million adherents in virtually every corner of the globe—including people from every nation, ethnic group, culture, profession, and social or economic class—it is probably the most diverse organized body of people on the planet today.

Its founder, Bahá'u'lláh, teaches that there is only one God, that there is only one human race, and that all the world's great religions represent stages in the progressive revelation of God's purpose for humankind. Bahá'ís believe that the unity of the entire human race is not only necessary for human progress but also inevitable. The Bahá'í Faith teaches, among other things, that religion should be a source of unity; condemns all forms of prejudice and racism; upholds the equality of women and men; confirms the importance and value of marriage and the family; establishes the need for the independent investigation of the truth; insists on access to education for all; asserts the essential harmony between science and religion;

declares the need to eliminate extremes of wealth and poverty; and exalts work done in a spirit of service to the level of worship.

Bahá'ís believe that religion should be a dynamic force that raises the individual, family, and community to new spiritual heights. To this end Bahá'ís all around the world work to create an atmosphere of love and unity in their own lives, in their families, and in their communities.

For more information about the Bahá'í Faith, visit

http://www.us.bahai.org/

or call

1-800-22-UNITE.

ABOUT BAHÁ'Í PUBLISHING

Bahá'í Publishing produces books based on the teachings of the Bahá'í Faith, a worldwide religious community united by the belief that there is one God, one human race, and one evolving religion.

For well over a century, Bahá'í communities around the globe have been working to break down barriers of prejudice between peoples and have collaborated with other like-minded groups to promote the model of a global society. At the heart of Bahá'í teachings is the conviction that humanity is a single people with a common destiny. In the words of Bahá'u'lláh, the Founder of the Bahá'í Faith, "The earth is but one country, and mankind its citizens."

Today the Bahá'í Faith is among the fastest growing of the world religions. With more than 5 million followers in at least 236 countries and dependent territories, it has already become the second most widespread of the world's faiths, surpassing every religion but Christianity in its geographic reach.

Bahá'í Publishing is an imprint of the Bahá'í Publishing Trust of the United States.

OTHER BOOKS AVAILABLE FROM BAHÁ'Í PUBLISHING

Refresh and Gladden My Spirit: Prayers and Meditations from Bahá'í Scripture

Introduction by Pamela Brode

Find hope, faith, and happiness in an uncertain world. Discover the Bahá'í approach to prayer with this collection of beautiful, soul-stirring prayers and meditations from Bahá'í scripture. Pamela Brode's introduction explains basic Bahá'í teachings on the subject of prayer and spiritual sustenance and considers questions such as What is prayer? Why pray? Are our prayers answered? Does prayer benefit the world? The selections that follow include more than 120 prayers and extracts from Bahá'í scripture on themes such as assistance from God, comfort, contentment, difficult times, death, faith, healing, marriage and family life, protection, strength, and many others. These powerful selections are sure to sustain, refresh, and gladden your spirit.